JULIA CHILD

JULIA CHILD

THE LAST INTERVIEW

and OTHER CONVERSATIONS

MELVILLE HOUSE
BROOKLYN · LONDON

JULIA CHILD: THE LAST INTERVIEW
AND OTHER CONVERSATIONS

"It's really a very easy recipe," an interview with Julia Child and Simone Beck, was first broadcast on *The Martha Deane Show* in October 1961 and is part of the audio and manuscript archives of radio station WOR-AM that were donated to the Library of Congress by RKO General, Inc.

"A Conversation with Julia Child, Spring 1984" by Sharon Hudgins appeared in *Gastronomica: The Journal of Critical Food Studies*, Vol. 5 no. 3, Summer 2005, pp. 104–108. © 2005 by the Regents of the University of California. Published by University of California Press.

"Julia Child" by Polly Frost originally appeared in the August 1989 issue of *Interview* magazine and was reprinted online on August 4, 2009.

"We knew a lot of fairly important people at that point" by Jewell Fenzi was conducted on November 7, 1991, as part of the Foreign Affairs Oral History Project, Foreign Service Spouse Series. Reprinted by permission of the Association for Diplomatic Studies and Training.

"I'm not a chef, I'm a teacher and a cook" conducted by Michael Rosen as part of *The Interviews: An Oral History of Television*, © Television Academy Foundation, June 25, 1999. Excerpt courtesy of the Television Academy Foundation Interviews, edited by Adrienne Faillace. See the full interview at TelevisionAcademy.com/Interviews.

"The Last Interview" by Wilbert Jones originally appeared as "A Chat with Julia Child" in *Prepared Foods* on September 1, 2004.

Melville House Publishing
46 John Street
Brooklyn, NY 11201

and

Melville House UK
Suite 2000 16/18 Woodford Rd
London E7 0H2

mhpbooks.com
@melvillehouse

ISBN: 978-1-61219-733-3
ISBN: 978-1-61219-734-0 (eBook)

Printed in the United States of America
10 9 8 7 6 5 4 3 2

A catalog record for this book is available from the Library of Congress.

CONTENTS

VII INTRODUCTION BY HELEN ROSNER

1 IT'S REALLY A VERY EASY RECIPE
Interview by Martha Deane
The Martha Deane Show
October 1961

33 A CONVERSATION WITH JULIA CHILD
Interview by Sharon Hudgins
Gastronomica: The Journal of Critical Food Studies
Spring 1984

51 JULIA CHILD
Interview by Polly Frost
Interview
August 1989

69 "WE KNEW A LOT OF FAIRLY IMPORTANT PEOPLE
AT THAT POINT"
Interview by Jewell Fenzi
The Foreign Affairs Oral History Project,
Foreign Service Spouse Series
November 7, 1991

103   **"I'M NOT A CHEF, I'M A TEACHER AND A COOK"**
Interview by Michael Rosen
Television Academy Foundation for *The Interviews: An
Oral History of Television*
June 25, 1999

137   **THE LAST INTERVIEW**
Interview by Wilbert Jones
Prepared Foods
September 1, 2004

Paul Child, who would become Julia's husband, first met her—the two were stationed together in 1944, in the Kandy, Ceylon branch of the Office of Strategic Services, the precursor to the Central Intelligence Agency—he described her in a letter to his brother as "a warm and witty girl" with a habit of gasping as she spoke. "Her slight atmosphere of hysteria," he wrote, "gets on my nerves." Years later, after they had fallen in love, and married, and their passion for one another had grown and deepened into an uncommonly rich and enduring devotion, Paul wrote a poem of love to her voice, describing her "mouth so sweet, so made for honeyed words."

The six interviews in this volume together tell a richly dimensional story of how Julia McWilliams—a talky California girl, intelligent and outgoing and a gawky six-foot-something—would grow to become Julia Child, a woman who stepped into her fame late enough in life that she was already formed, already confident in her height and voice and manner, already richly content in her life with Paul. Even in her earliest public appearances, as in the 1961 radio interview with *The Martha Deane Show*, where she and Simone Beck discuss the creation of the first volume of *Mastering the Art of French Cooking*, there's a preview of the Julia to come—the jokes and playfulness, but also her forceful evangelism for the notion that the best results come from the best product and the best method. Often this meant techniques that might appear at first to be bizarre, or flat-out wrong, but which reveal themselves to be exquisite models of efficiency and grace. "When you first do it, it doesn't seem the right way to do it," Julia tells Deane of the French method for fluting mushrooms, which involves holding the blade steady, while turning the fungus. "But you learn that it is the right way. That the mushroom is cutting itself against the knife. And it's very pretty."

When she appeared in the homes of television-owning Americans in 1963, Julia was both an oddity—the voice! Her height! The relative novelty of an instructional cooking show!—and an instant, magnetic success. Already famous as the co-author of *Mastering the Art of French Cooking*, which had been published to wild acclaim two years earlier, Julia's television career seems, in retrospect, like an inevitability: Her charisma, her extraordinary knowledge of cuisine, and her natural talent as a teacher, all of which had been instrumental in the success of the book, were seemingly tailor-made for the camera. *The French Chef*, produced by Boston public television station WGBH and distributed nationwide, was a sensation. It ran for ten years, airing over two hundred episodes, each of them just Julia: a solid thirty minutes of her swooping voice and her strong arms, conversationally delivering to the viewer a precise and foolproof method to make *quiche*, or *pot-au-feu*, or a whole three-course ham dinner for guests in under half an hour. She was the most famous French chef in the world—despite not being French, nor (as she insisted, futilely, for her entire life) a proper chef.

There's no shortage of chronicles of Julia's extraordinary impact on American gastronomy. Through her books and television shows she almost single-handedly changed the way we ate, leading home cooks out of a post-war industrial stasis of canned vegetables and E-Z-meal efficiency. In advocating for a French way of cooking she promoted seasonal vegetables, good dairy, and whole ingredients; to the tired rituals of making and eating dinner, she reintroduced a pleasure that wartime and its attendant industries had stripped away. Over the years she shared the stage (figuratively and often literally) with culinary titans like James Beard, M.F.K. Fisher, Craig Claiborne, and Jacques Pepin, but among them Julia was the best known, the most influential, the most beloved—"The most famous cook in the world!" declared the cover of *Julia Child's Menu Cookbook*. When Julia went on television and told her viewers to start tonight's dinner with a nice whole duck, or lovely fresh artichokes, butchers and grocers would be sold out in an hour.

Her story has been told so many times it takes on the smoothed-out shape of legend. A college graduate who worked in advertising when World War II began and wanted to do her bit, but she turned out to be too tall for the WACs and the WAVEs (the women's military units), so she volunteered for the OSS. There, she was stationed in Ceylon (now Sri Lanka), where she had full security clearance and was, if not quite a spy, certainly well-sourced in various secrets. Before the OSS Julia had felt at loose ends (she was unmarried at the decrepit old age of thirty-two, and was nursing dashed hopes of becoming a writer) but in her new job she found both a thrilling vocational competence, and—in Paul Child, a cartographer and aesthete ten years her senior—a soul-sweeping love affair. They both ended up transferred from Kandy to Kunming, in China, where their romance blossomed. After the war, they returned to America; they spent some time apart, and then some time together, and then they got married, and then they moved to France.

And then they moved to France. In Kunming, Julia had become enamored of Chinese cuisine—Yunnan province was, she recalled in her memoirs, the place where her palate had first truly awakened. "The Chinese food was wonderful, and we ate out as often as we could. That is when I became interested in food," she wrote, rhapsodizing about the joyous rituals of Chinese banquet dining, the extraordinary range of flavors, and—not least—the culinary sophistication of everyone around her, Chinese and American alike. It's hard not to wonder what would have happened if Julia and Paul Child had remained in Kunming, or if Paul had been sent to Tokyo instead of Paris, or to Bangkok, or Delhi, or any of the other capitals of great cuisine. How would the world have changed? Would a wok or a *handi* have become ubiquitous in American kitchens, the way omelette pans and boning knives are now? But Paris is what it was: the Foreign Service sent the Childs to France, where Paul worked in the U.S. embassy, and Julia was left to find a way to fill her days. She ended up at Le Cordon Bleu, in a morning class taught entirely in French and attended entirely by Americans, and the rest, as they say, is history.

For most of Julia's public life she maintained an apolitical mien, but in her later years, she spoke more openly about her liberal politics, holding forth on the lingering evils of McCarthyism, the ongoing immorality of the Republican party, and the fundamental necessity of the feminist and pro-choice movements. In this volume's 1989 interview with journalist Polly Frost, from *Interview* magazine: "I don't think this administration seems interested in doing anything about the environment. These people are anti-abortion, but they're not doing anything for the future." Or two years later, speaking with Jewell Fenzi for *Foreign Affairs'* fascinating project of taking oral histories of the spouses of Foreign Service officers, an eighty-one-year-old Julia says of her involvements, "the American Institute of Wine and Food, that's mostly what I do now. That, and I am very much interested in Planned Parenthood, and Smith College, and the Democratic Party."

Julia's political fierceness wasn't something she came to late in life. As the wife of a career civil servant, and a former intelligence worker herself, she stayed well informed and was unafraid to be vocal. In 2013, the historian Helen Horowitz uncovered among Julia's papers a blistering letter written in 1954, while Julia was living in Paris and immersed in *Mastering the Art*. It was to Aloise Buckley Heath, a fellow Smith alumna and the sister of William F. Buckley, Jr., the prominent conservative author and defender of McCarthyism. Heath had written urging Child and other Smith graduates to withhold donations until the college had sacked five professors suspected of being communists. An enraged Julia replied, "In the blood-heat of pursuing the enemy, many people are forgetting what we are fighting for. We are fighting for our hard-won liberty and our freedom; for our Constitution and the due processes of our laws; and for the right to differ in ideas, religion and politics. I am convinced that in your zeal to fight against our enemies, you, too, have forgotten what you are fighting for."*

I think about this letter often (what would Julia think about the darkness of America today?), and in particular I come back again and again to Julia's fiery closing paragraph:

---

* Horowitz, Helen Lefkowitz. "The politics of Julia Child '34," *Smith Alumnae Quarterly*, Spring 2013. https://alumnae.smith.edu/smithstories/the-politics-of-julia-child-34/.

"I am sending to Smith College in this same mail, along with a copy of this letter, a check to duplicate my annual contribution to the Alumnae Fund. I am confident that our Trustees and our President know what they are doing. They are only too well aware of the dangers of totalitarianism, as it is always the great institutions of learning that are attacked first in any police state. For the colleges harbor the 'dangerous' people, the people who know how to think, whose minds are free."*

I never met Julia Child, though I saw her once, from far away, making her way across a grassy lawn. It was my sophomore year at Smith College, where I matriculated some seventy years behind Julia—she was one of the institution's most luminous alumnae, certainly our most famous, and despite being, at the time, in her late eighties, she had made the trip down the Massachusetts Turnpike from her home in Cambridge to visit her alma mater. News of her arrival rippled across campus—she had sat in on someone's French seminar, she had been spotted entering Hubbard House, her own old red-brick dormitory, for a dining-hall lunch. I was rushing to an afternoon philosophy class when I saw her, moving slowly with age but smiling at the students and aides who buzzed around her, and I remember marveling to myself: "Julia Child—she's real!"

At that time, in 2001, cooking as a widespread artistic hobby was just on the cusp of being truly in vogue. Modern food culture—with its built-in assumption that things like obsessive ingredient provenance and fine details of technique

---

*   Ibid.

are of universal interest—was ascendant, but not yet at critical mass. My micro-generation was the last, I think, where it was still something of an oddity for a teenager to throw a dinner party, though now it's unremarkable for young adults to approach the preparation of dinner with the same adolescent solemnity previously reserved for composing world-weary poems, or practicing guitar in public. I had earned some mild infamy at my lunch table for using a juice glass to whip together vinaigrettes for my salad-bar greens, which was about as far as things went. "I wonder if Julia would like my dressing," I had said to a friend, earlier that day. She rolled her eyes at me. "Julia likes everything," she said.

Julia, despite her effervescent personality, did not actually like everything, though I understand what my friend meant: the Julia who appeared on our televisions and in the pages of our cookbooks (and, for some of us, on the sidewalks crisscrossing the college lawns) almost always wore the sunny, encouraging expression of a favorite teacher, the sort of person who believes in you, who laughs off your failures while praising your effort. In fact, she considered herself to be a teacher, first and foremost—and from the start: During the ten-year period that she and co-authors Simone Beck and Louisette Bertholle were writing the first volume of *Mastering the Art of French Cooking*, it was Julia who insisted that the book be instructional, rather than just a collection of recipes, and it was that meticulous, conversational instruction that catapulted *Mastering the Art* to its instant status as an indispensable classic.

What didn't Julia like? More than anything, she loathed

snobbery—though with her patrician upbringing and Francophilia she was often caricatured as a snob herself, she labored endlessly to rid French cuisine of its reputation as haughty and upper-crust, and avoided fussy equipment and the word "gourmet." (She preferred the much more egalitarian phrases "good cooking" and "good cuisine.") She loathed cilantro. She was endlessly frustrated by people who gave up on cooking because they refused to follow instructions, or who wouldn't put in the effort to get the proper result. She famously disdained the 2003 blog "The Julie/Julia Project," in which writer Julie Powell cooked her way through all of *Mastering the Art.* ("I've heard of her," she sniffed of Powell to *The New York Times.* "I haven't read any of her stuff.") She also, to my great delight, hated bottled salad dressing—in her 1999 conversation with Michael Rosen, in this collection, an extraordinarily detailed account of her television career, she says, "I don't believe in bottled salad dressing . . . why should you have it bottled? It's so easy to make. And they never use very good oil."

As I said, nobody talks like Julia Child. In her hundreds of hours of television, in the thousands of pages of her books, in her magazine columns, while dining at restaurants, at private dinners, in letters to friends, across the table from reporters, with her loved ones, she was a person who found her greatest self in having something to say, and saying it frankly. The Julia we know is not soft-spoken or demure, not prettily laying the table, not blank-faced and blinking in the spotless, appliance-sponsored kitchen of tomorrow. She is telling stories, explaining techniques, recalling in

"IT'S REALLY A VERY EASY RECIPE"

INTERVIEW WITH MARTHA DEANE
THE MARTHA DEANE SHOW
OCTOBER 1961

MARTHA DEANE: It's 10:15 in New York, and this is Martha Deane, and good morning everybody. And again, I'm glad you're with us because our guests are two interesting women who live in various places and travel in various places and cook in various places, and the kind of cooking they do . . . we all should be able to cook like that.

And now here are Julia Child and Simone Beck, the two authors of the superb cookbook *Mastering the Art of French Cooking*. I'm delighted to have the both of you on the program. Good morning.

JULIA CHILD: Good morning.

DEANE: Mrs. Child, I thought you might like to tell our listeners about this book in a general way. Some of the things you were telling me were that, really, it's a book of French cooking, but it's for the American cook, and it's for the woman who doesn't have servants.

CHILD: It's also for men too. It's for anyone who really loves to cook and likes to eat and does all their own cooking and serving, and we've tried to make it absolutely foolproof so that every recipe is supposed to work. Because I think in some books you feel that you're dumb if the dish doesn't come out the way you'd like it to, but our feeling is that in that case, it's the *book* that's bad. And these are all supposed to—well, they all *do* work because we've tried them out ourselves, and all of our pupils have.

DEANE: They've been tried out many times on many people.

CHILD: Many times.

DEANE: Madame Beck, tell our listeners that wonderful story about the number of times you try out recipes, and usually on your husband first, and then you try them out on other people, I gather.

SIMONE BECK: Well, my husband has very good taste, see, so sometimes when I am not sure of myself, well, he has to taste. So three times, four times, six times, then I think, *Now it's okay*, but still you must work again. So I do it again, and at the end of the week, he says, "Well, never give me another—another dish the same because, you see, now I have had plenty." [*Laughter*]

DEANE: Well, one of the fine recipes in the book *Mastering the Art of French Cooking* is the scalloped potatoes with cream.

CHILD: Yes.

DEANE: And you told me before we started broadcasting that your husband ate scalloped potatoes with cream every day for six days.

BECK: Every day. Every day!

DEANE: And the seventh day, he said it was all right?

BECK: Yes, and now you can do the recipe. So, once it was okay, I sent it to Mrs. Child, and again, she tried it to see if it was okay for her. See? That's why the book could be, I think, good, because I think the recipe was all taste. I don't know how many times each recipe was tried and tried again.

DEANE: When I think of poor Mr. Beck over seven days with scalloped potatoes and cream, I'll bet he has not looked at a potato or a bit of cream since.

CHILD: Probably not. [*Laughter*]

DEANE: Now, Madame Beck said that she then sent the recipe to you, Julia Child. So maybe then this is a good point to tell us about your collaboration and how you two met and what happened. And then you've also mentioned somewhere along the line running schools, plural. So let's talk first about the collaboration, *Mastering the Art of French Cooking*, and then we can talk about the schools later.

CHILD: Well Madame Beck and I met about . . . heavens, in 1950, I think it was. We had a mutual friend who knew that we were both very much interested in cooking.

DEANE: Was this in Paris?

CHILD: This was in Paris. We were living there at that point. We lived there for six years.

DEANE: Your husband was in the diplomatic service.

CHILD: Yes, he was. He was at the embassy in Paris. He was running exhibits. And we don't have any children, and I've always liked food, so I went to the Cordon Bleu. And at that time, the GIs had the GI Bill of Rights, so I joined a class at the Cordon Bleu starting at seven in the morning. And I went there for about six months, and after we'd made *chaudfroid de poulet* and *homard à l'américaine* about six or eight times, I felt that was enough, and I wanted to do something else. And just then, I met Madame Beck and we really fell into each other's arms. She was interested in doing a French cookbook for America, and I was beginning to think that might interest me. And then, we had some American friends who came over to Paris, and they wanted to learn cooking, so I think within two days we started our cooking school, L'École de Trois Gourmandes. And it went on all the rest of the time we were in Paris. And then when we moved to Marseille, Madame Beck and Madame Bertholle kept on with the cooking school in Paris. And then finally when my husband and I moved to Washington, I established a branch there. And then my husband was moved to Norway as cultural attaché, and I started a cooking school there, L'École de Trois Gourmandes. And Madam Beck has always had hers in Paris. And now . . .

DEANE: And she still has it.

CHILD: And she still has it. Wherever either of us are, we always establish a cooking school.

DEANE: Well, you establish a school just like that?

CHILD: Well, it's very easy, I've found, to do. All you do, you get some prospective customers, and you ask them over for lunch. And I have a lunch that I always give them, which is a little—I give them a little *pâte à choux* with chopped mushrooms and cream and a little Madeira in it and then a poached egg and a *sauce béarnaise* and that always slays them. And then we have a lovely cake of Madame Beck's chocolate almond cake. It's one of the best cakes I ever ate.

DEANE: I read that recipe in the book.

CHILD: We have that for dessert, and then after that, I have as many pupils as I want.

DEANE: They all say, "We want to learn to make these."

CHILD: Yes, mm-hmm. That's all.

DEANE: And where do you start cooking then?

CHILD: Well we've—

DEANE: I think of a school as having, you know, a special stove and a special—

CHILD: Well, I have a rather special kitchen. It's nice and large, and I have a restaurant stove, and if the pupils came and cooked there then they'd say, "Oh, well, I won't be able to cook at home because she has all this fancy equipment." So I've found it's better for people to gather in their own group, and then we go from house to house each week. We go to someone else's house, and they're cooking on their own stove. And then we always have a delicious lunch with a little wine, and it's a great deal of fun because they're cooking with the people they like. It's much more fun all around.

BECK: And you get to say—

CHILD: Excuse me? What?

BECK: You're counting their utensils.

CHILD: I always go in and inspect the kitchen first.

BECK: Yes, see how it is.

CHILD: If they don't have the utensils they need—we need—I bring them along in my big French shopping bag, which is right over there. Usually their knives aren't sharp, so I always bring a lot of knives along.

DEANE: You make a big point of that in the book. Keep the knives sharp.

CHILD: Well, you can't do anything with a dull knife.

DEANE: This is very important for the cook, isn't it?

BECK: Yes, well it's important for everything. Without a sharp enough knife, you don't cut properly. You cannot cut properly.

CHILD: And there's lots of cutting in French cooking, you've got to learn how to do it quickly. That's the dog work. For instance, if you were an apprentice cook in Paris, you usually would start out at fourteen. You'd spend two years learning how to prepare vegetables, cutting, doing all the dog work. But you don't have to spend two years learning it.

BECK: No.

CHILD: As a person, I mean, I learned it in about two weeks of just hard work. Or how to flute a mushroom. That takes a little while. Finally, you get on to how to do it. But you have to do all these things quickly, or you just spend so much time on it that you're not getting to the actual cooking.

DEANE: How do you flute a mushroom?

CHILD: Well, you hold the cap of the mushroom in your hands with your thumb on it. And then you have a very sharp knife, which you hold rigidly, then you turn the mushroom against the knife and it takes off just a little flute, or edge.

DEANE: The trick is in turning the mushroom rather than the knife.

CHILD: Yes, you start at the crown and then you rub the mushroom against the rigidly held knife. But the knife has to be sharp.

BECK: Very sharp. The corners. Very sharp.

DEANE: That's wonderful. I'm so glad I asked.

CHILD: [*laughs*] Well, it's not difficult. When you first do it, it doesn't seem the right way to do it. But you learn that it is the right way. That the mushroom is cutting itself against the knife. And it's very pretty.

DEANE: That reminds me of something else in the book. The trick there obviously is to move the mushroom and not the knife.

CHILD: Yes, exactly.

DEANE: In a wonderful recipe for a cake, I don't have it in front of us, so I'll see if I can remember which one. I think it's one of the orange cakes. Anyway, chopped almonds are put all around the sides. Am I right? Now, you stop me—I'm just trying to remember. And instead of sprinkling the almonds on the cake, or, you know, dropping them around the edge, you put them in a pan after they've been slivered, chopped— what do you say, slivered?

CHILD: Pulverized. Powdered.

DEANE: And you hold the cake.

CHILD: Yeah.

DEANE: And roll it against the almonds.

CHILD: You hold the cake in the flat of your hand like that, and then you just brush the almonds against it.

DEANE: Rather than just sprinkling them on.

CHILD: Not so . . . if you did it in a plate, then you'd get almonds all over, and then you'd have to put on a decoration of leaves to hide the mess you've made. Well, if you hold it in your hand, you can just slip it on.

DEANE: But I noticed a great many things in there. Maybe that's what's been wrong with me. A great many things are just done the opposite of . . .

CHILD: Well, these are all of the French professional and chef techniques. And they're much easier, and they have to do things the easiest way.

DEANE: Now, Madame Beck do you teach cooking in Paris the same way Mrs. Child does, going to people's homes?

BECK: Exactly the same way because we are working together, and of course it would be the same way. We teach, you see? Young girls and sometimes not so young and even older, old women. Doesn't matter. They even can learn at sixty, even seventy years old. It doesn't matter if they want to learn something.

DEANE: Women who've decided they're tired of the cooking they've been doing and just want to get better?

BECK: Well, sometimes—

CHILD: They want to have fun too.

BECK: Sometimes they have no servants, no cooks, so they say, "Well, one day, I must know how to do something properly," you see. So even if they're old, they will do it themselves.

DEANE: Now, Mrs. Child just said something interesting— this is for people who want to have fun. And that's really the point of the whole thing, isn't it? Let me do a shopping list I brought along, and then let's start right there of why you said this is for people who want to have fun.

• • •

DEANE: Our guests are Simone Beck and Julia Child, the two authors of a superb cookbook, as I told you, *Mastering the Art of French Cooking.* And just before I interrupted with that shopping list, Mrs. Child, you had said this is for people who want to have fun. And I think I said that's the point of the whole thing of being a good cook, isn't it, because if you don't enjoy it and don't like it, it's very difficult to be a good cook. And certainly very difficult to do French cooking, isn't it?

CHILD: I think, too, that you enjoy it much more if you know what you're doing. If you're sort of at sea and don't really know quite how to do things, you can't enjoy it. For instance, I sew terribly, and if I ever took some lessons, I might like it, but to me, sewing is just agony. But I think with cooking, you have to have instruction and training so that things are going to turn out properly. Because if you have one failure after another, you become psychotic, don't you think?

DEANE: Well, I guess so.

CHILD: [*laughs*] I guess so? Madame Beck seems to agree with you. [*Laughter.*]

DEANE: The important thing, though, that I ought to bring up is that a great many American women, American cooks, are sort of scared of this French cooking, a little frightened, I suspect, of the title *Mastering the Art of French Cooking*, because most of us think of this as being very much more difficult than our cooking. And early in the book you warn against shortcuts so it does take more time.

BECK: No, not more time, really. I don't think so. If you know exactly, if you read the recipe very carefully. I think it's not more time.

CHILD: I would agree, I don't think it's more time.

BECK: I think the end result is so magnificent that you—

DEANE: Well, I guess the reason I bring that up is that a lot of sayings in this country now seem to me geared to time saving. Everything is, as you know, "Do it this way because it saves time." And then, "Do it that way because it saves time." Frankly, I don't know what people will do with all this time they allegedly save, but it does, don't you agree, it does seem to be kind of a—

CHILD: Depends on what you like to do. If you like to play bridge, you like to spend the time on it; if you like to cook, nothing is too much trouble. Unless you have eight children and laundry and something else to do, then you probably wouldn't do a very complicated meal. But if it's your pleasure, if it's like going out to play golf, you love to do it, and you want to do it well.

DEANE: Now let's talk about some of the specific things in the book. I think our listeners might like to hear some of the things you've written about buffet suppers, for example, because from now on to the holidays, a great many people entertain a great deal, and buffet is a nice way to do it and, sometimes, an easier way to do it. And I like some of the recipes you give for buffet suppers ever so much. I think that sometimes people get so tired of the roast turkey and the baked ham on the buffet table and would like to do something else. And indeed you've done some wonderful things, such as the beef stew in red wine, which, you say in the book, would be good for buffet suppers.

CHILD: Oh, excellent for buffets. One of the good things about it is that you can do it, well, two days ahead of time, and it just is steeping in its wine and sauce. It picks up flavor and is just even better if you do it ahead.

DEANE: Do it two days ahead and put it in the icebox.

CHILD: Perfectly well, and then it just needs a little reheating up until it's hot through. And the chicken, the *coq au vin*, same thing.

DEANE: Same thing. Chicken in red wine.

CHILD: What do you think about the veal scallops and cream and mushrooms?

BECK: I think it's a very fine dish. And so easy to—

DEANE: For a buffet?

BECK: Yes, why not? And it's very easy to do.

CHILD: Of course, veal is rather expensive. If you wanted to save money, you might want to do something like chicken, which is always inexpensive, such as a cold chicken and lemon jelly. And that's very easy. There's no browning or anything like that.

BECK: I think that's marvelous. Anybody can make this dish.

CHILD: And you can use an old hen if you want.

BECK: An old hen, an old guinea hen, an old pheasant, yes?

CHILD: Or just an old hen–type hen.

BECK: An old hen type, yes. It's a wonderful, wonderful dish.

DEANE: That's an old hen–type hen. That's our Mrs. Child isn't it? [*Laughter.*]

CHILD: Well, as for other inexpensive things, lamb stew is very inexpensive too.

DEANE: Now we better sort of do one of these. Let's see, let's tell them. Do you want to talk? Do you want to do the chicken and lemon jelly? Do you want to talk about that?

CHILD: Why don't we talk about the beef stew one because everyone seems to like that?

DEANE: All right, beef stew and red wine.

CHILD: Beef is the most popular meat, isn't it?

DEANE: Yes, I think so. Now, that one's on page 315 in case everybody's looking for its place. I want you to know that each of us has her own cookbook right here this morning. I have paper clips on mine but you all found yours first.

CHILD: This recipe covers a page and a half. This is large print of course, but you find after you've done it once, you'll probably never have to look at the recipe again because it's very simple. All you do is brown the meat, and you'll note it's interesting that very often American recipes, if you're going to brown the meat, you flour the meat first and brown it, but that's not French. For the French browning, you'd have to dry the meat, and you brown that first, and that gives a particular flavor to the meat.

DEANE: But you dry the meat first.

CHILD: You always have to dry it because you have to let the fat out, the meat dry, or nothing's going to brown. It's just going to stick to the bottom of the pan. So it's really a very easy recipe, but we've given it many details so that you don't miss something like drying the meat. But once you've done it, you really wouldn't have to look at the recipe again. You might forget about how many cups of things, but for this kind of a recipe, doesn't make too much difference how many cups of wine or bouillon you have. You always taste the sauce after you've done it, and you add whatever else is necessary.

DEANE: Now, I've noticed that all through the book, you've recommended doing all kinds of stews in the oven rather than on top of the stove. Do you always do that, Madame Beck?

BECK: I always do it.

CHILD: But you don't have to, do you?

BECK: Of course not. But I think it's easier for a housewife who is doing something in her house. By putting a covered casserole in the oven, she can do what the kids are doing and come back. She can do it carefully, you see. Her cooking is going very slowly. It won't burn.

CHILD: That's what they call the *mijoter*, or simmering. That's very French country household cooking.

BECK: It's very easy.

DEANE: But you do all kinds of stews. All the meat and the chicken and the fowl.

CHILD: But you can do it on top; it just means you have to watch it a little bit more, unless you have an absolutely regulated top. But you have to have a very heavy casserole on the top because in the oven you have enveloping even heat, so it really cooks a little quicker and more evenly in the oven than it does on top, but you can do it either way.

DEANE: So you can do that for twenty or thirty people a couple of days ahead?

CHILD: Oh, sure.

DEANE: And that would really take care of the supper.

CHILD: Oh, yeah. And if you wanted an easier one than this, the beef *bourguignonne* is one that's called a *civet*. Oh, it's the *daube*. You just put everything in the pot and just cook it. It doesn't have as fine a taste, but it's an awfully easy and nice one to do. So if you're in a hurry, all you need to do is cut up all your vegetables, and you roll the meat in the flour, and you put it in layers in the pot, stick it in the oven, and that's it. The daube is very easy.

BECK: Same way.

CHILD: One thing about the care that you take in making the beef bourguignonne is that it makes it one of the best beef stews there is. The daube, as you find when you make one and then the other, is awfully good, but it doesn't have the sophistication of the bourguignonne.

BECK: And when you know how to do the beef bourguignonne, you know how to do the coq au vin. It's exactly the same way. Stick it in red wine.

DEANE: It's the same recipe.

BECK: Same way, how to do it.

CHILD: In other words, once you've learned one, you can do any kind of a stew. Probably not a mackerel stew. [*Laughter.*]

DEANE: Mackerel stew? This is rather revolting.

BECK: A fish, exactly. A Spanish dish.

CHILD: The idea doesn't sound very good. [*Laughter.*]

DEANE: I go along with you on nearly everything, but you bring up these things that I don't go along with, and I'm just not going to play.

CHILD: All right.

DEANE: You better tell about cold fowl and lemon jelly. Because Madame Beck thinks that is obviously one of her favorite recipes of the book.

BECK: Yes.

CHILD: She developed it. It's her recipe.

BECK: It's my recipe because one day, my husband brings some old pheasant—an old partridge—home, and he asks what can I do with it, you see, to make it good. And I think this is a wonderful recipe, you see, because even with an old pheasant, even with an old partridge, or even an old guinea hen, you can have a wonderful cold dish with lemon jelly. Because with some olive oil, you cook, you see, and it goes in the flesh. Lemon slices—

DEANE: You cook the old fowl in olive oil.

BECK: Everything is cooked in a pot, see. And covered with vegetables. Then slices of lemon, oil—olive oil, if you have it. Olive oil is always better. White wine—dry white wine— and pimento, and all kinds of vegetables, and it's cooked for only two hours; that's all. And after everything, let it cool, remove the grease, put it in a pot, like a large bowl, and the day after, even on the night after, it is a wonderful cold dish for a buffet.

CHILD: It just Jell-Os by itself. The lemon helps it jelly.

BECK: The lemon, the bones, all the ingredients, you see, are cooking very slowly together.

CHILD: It's just a fancy thing with very little effort.

BECK: No, nothing. Anybody could make that recipe, anybody; a child could make it. You put everything in a pot and nothing else.

CHILD: Let her go.

BECK: Let her go. Only you need to have the good ingredients, you see, that's all. There's no mystery there. There's no *tour de main*, we say in French, you see. That's a trick.

CHILD: As you notice, Madame Beck has recommended a white wine, but we find that because white wine in the States is rather expensive, white vermouth works extremely well.

BECK: Yes, wonderful! Dry vermouth.

CHILD: It's much better than a sour, bad white wine. You don't use very much of it. In fact, you use less than you would a white wine.

BECK: Dry vermouth can always replace dry white wine, it's better.

DEANE: Is that true in any recipe, Madame Beck?

BECK: Yes, of course.

CHILD: We've put them all in the book.

DEANE: Use dry vermouth instead of white wine.

BECK: [*looking in book*] Here, half a cup dry white wine, one third cup dry white vermouth.

DEANE: Well, that'll take care of that old guinea hen or whatever.

BECK: It's very important, you see, because everyone can have dry vermouth. Dry white wine has peps.

CHILD: It's too expensive.

BECK: Expensive, yes, difficult to arrange, yes.

DEANE: Now, let me finish that shopping list that I brought along, and then let's get to the dessert department because there's a wonderful dessert department in this fine book of yours, *Mastering the Art of French Cooking.*

• • •

DEANE: And now we get back to our guests, Simone Beck and Julia Child, two of the three authors of this fine new cookbook, *Mastering the Art of French Cooking.* And I think we agreed to get into the dessert department, and perhaps we could persuade Madame Beck to tell us about her famous chocolate cake, do you think?

CHILD: Yes, so good.

DEANE: How she does it, and why it's so good.

BECK: Well, it's very easy again, very easy cake to make.

DEANE: But you say that about everything.

BECK: Yes, well, it's easy. When you know about cooking, everything is easy. Do it once, and you can do it all your life. Even without reading the book. You know it by your heart and by your taste. Well, this is a very good chocolate cake, and the trick I think for this cake is to be overcooked.

DEANE: Overcooked?

BECK: Overcooked!

CHILD: Undercooked.

BECK: Undercooked. That's not to be overcooked, it has to be undercooked. [*Laughter*]

DEANE: Here, let me do it for you: the trick in this chocolate cake is to undercook it.

BECK: Undercook it. [*Laughter*]

DEANE: No, that's all right. Don't worry about it. You can imagine how I'd give a recipe for chocolate cake if I were in Paris and you were interviewing me on French radio! Just hold that thought, and you'll feel better about everything.

CHILD: Well, this is the cake that has the almonds and the butter in it.

BECK: Yes, almond butter chocolate, and the chocolate is melted with a little bit of coffee.

DEANE: Madame Beck, the thing that interested me is that you don't use baking powder, you use egg whites to make the cake light.

BECK: Never baking powder.

DEANE: No baking powder in cake?

BECK: No, no. Some cakes use it, of course. Some.

DEANE: But not your cakes.

BECK: Not in France, you see. When you make an Alsatian cake like *kouglof*, you use some special flour.

DEANE: But for your chocolate cake and your orange cake and your almond, you use egg whites—

BECK: Egg whites.

DEANE: Instead of baking powder.

BECK: Never baking powder.

DEANE: You both do an amazing bit in the book on egg whites. I think we ought to talk about egg whites a little.

CHILD: Well, egg whites are awfully important in *soufflés* and desserts. You have to have them. Now, when you beat an egg white, it has to rise seven times its original volume. It has to be absolutely smooth, and when you hold up a bit of egg white in the beater, it makes a little point that folds over at the top. But it has to be smooth and velvety. And it can't and it shouldn't have those granules in it. Once it has the granules, it means that some of its puffing quality has broken down.

DEANE: First, you warn in the book against using a bowl that has ever had grease in it.

CHILD: Mm-hmm. That seems to hold the egg whites—

DEANE: You apparently have a special bowl for beating eggs.

CHILD: Well, in France you have a lovely round-bottom, un-lined, copper bowl. But if you bought that in this country it would cost you twenty-five dollars. We found just by chance that a plastic bowl works almost as well as a copper bowl. It's something chemical, and I don't know what it is, but I think it's that the egg whites sort of cling to the copper, which allows them to rise up more. I don't know what the chemical reason is.

DEANE: Maybe then you could recommend to my listeners a plastic bowl.

CHILD: A plastic bowl and a great big handheld whip is best, but if you don't have the muscles in your arms and some people, women, do not, you can use a handheld electric beater. But you have to hold it a certain—

DEANE: It has to be handheld.

CHILD: Yes, because you have to circulate as much air as possible into the egg whites. So you circulate the beater all around and you go rather slowly at first until they begin to foam. And then you turn it on to about medium. But then you keep circulating it and as soon as you stop the beater, hold it up and the egg whites stand in little stiff peaks that just folds over on the top. They're stiff, and that's it.

DEANE: And that's what you use in this cake instead of baking powder?

CHILD: Yes. But some plastic bowls have a slight oiliness on. I got one in Boston the other day, and it was polyethylene or something—or poly-something or other. I don't know.

DEANE: Poly-something. They're all poly-something.

CHILD: Well this one worked all right. But if you find a bowl, a plastic bowl, that doesn't work, you just go and buy another one. They don't cost much.

DEANE: And save that bowl just for eggs.

CHILD: You don't want it to get oily because it does absorb oil.

BECK: There's a stick on the edge, see, because a copper basin sticks on the edge. If you slip down like in Pyrex, it's no good, you see. It has to be on the edges.

CHILD: On the edges. It's just as if you're making a puff pastry, you wet the pastry sheet first to make the puff pastry hold on to it, so it has a footing and can pull up and rise from the footing.

DEANE: Are you good at making puff pastry too?

CHILD: Yes, but we find that American flour is a little different than French. It takes much more time because American flour is hard wheat and is rubbery—you have to rest it, usually about two hours between the rolls.

DEANE: Well, now, I know the name of an American flour that's not. And when we stop the broadcasting I will give you both some names.

CHILD: We've written to some flour companies, but we'd like to know a name.

DEANE: I think I know one.

CHILD: They don't sell soft wheat flour to the ordinary person, which is too bad because it's much better for pastry.

BECK: Too dry, you see. In France, the flour is moist.

DEANE: Madame Beck, what other kinds of desserts do you like to make besides cakes?

BECK: Well I always like *charlotte*. It's very popular in France, you see. *Charlotte aux pommes*. It's very nice and a very easy recipe.

CHILD: That lovely recipe of yours—the *charlotte malakoff*, which has lady fingers with this buttery almond crème inside.

BECK: And you could put strawberry and raspberry in between, you see. That's very, very—

CHILD: Not a slimming dessert. You just take a little bit, but—my, it's good.

BECK: The very popular *charlotte aux pommes*.

CHILD: With apple, apple *charlotte*—

BECK: Apple of Bellevue.

CHILD: Yes.

BECK: That's very, very good.

CHILD: Very good.

BECK: Very good recipe.

DEANE: Easy to do, I have no doubt. She says everything's easy.

BECK: It is easy.

CHILD: Well, once you know how to do these things, it isn't difficult because you're doing the same thing all the time, but you just make different combinations.

BECK: Mixing egg whites and sugar, it's the base of making the cakes. When you know how it has to go—

DEANE: You mean how to mix sugar with egg yolks—

BECK: The sugar and egg yolk, you must work very often. Very often you begin to make your cake, mixing egg yolks and sugar.

CHILD: Beating.

BECK: Beating until its pale yellow and running like a ribbon.

CHILD: Makes the ribbon as they always say.

BECK: It makes a ribbon when you run it with your spoon, like that, falling like a ribbon, it's right.

DEANE: Now you keep on beating the egg yolk and sugar until it makes a ribbon when you bring it up out of the bowl on a spoon.

BECK: When it falls back like ribbon, see.

CHILD: That takes maybe a minute.

BECK: A minute, yes.

CHILD: Then you take an electric mixer.

BECK: That's very easy.

CHILD: Then you have to know how to beat your egg whites, but that's easy to do. And you have to know how to fold, and that's easy to do.

BECK: And fold this chocolate cake.

DEANE: Well you have a diagram in the book on folding in the egg whites.

CHILD: Oh, yes, and we have a picture of what the egg whites should look like when they are done.

DEANE: Because you fold the egg whites in with a rubber spatula—

CHILD: Mm-hmm.

DEANE: By cutting while the egg white is poured on, first you put a tiny bit in.

CHILD: To lighten the thing up. What you want is to fold in the egg whites carefully so that you don't deflate them. You have to keep as much of their volume as possible so that when it gets in the oven, it's going to act as a puff.

DEANE: After you add in a little to lighten it, you pour on the rest of the egg white—

CHILD: You scrape them on because they don't pour on that thing, and then you come down, slowly down, with your spatula and out and up, and it brings just a little bit of the egg white down and a little bit of the mixture up over, and that is done very quickly. And that is terribly important because you can beat—

DEANE: For a soufflé.

CHILD: For anything.

BECK: Anything—even for a cake it's the same way, it's the same thing.

DEANE: I wish we had more time—

CHILD: Those are easy too, you just have to—

BECK: Know about it, you see.

CHILD: Or be shown or read the book.

BECK: Read the book, and you'll know everything.

DEANE: I wish we had more time because this has been delightful, and I thank you both ever so much for coming. And I want to tell our listeners that our guests have been this morning Simone Beck and Julia Child, the authors of a fine new cookbook, *Mastering the Art of French Cooking.*

A CONVERSATION WITH JULIA CHILD

INTERVIEW WITH SHARON HUDGINS
*GASTRONOMICA: THE JOURNAL OF CRITICAL
FOOD STUDIES*
SPRING 1984

In the Spring of 1984, the American military newspaper in Europe, the *Stars and Stripes*, sent me from my home base in Munich to interview Julia Child in Paris. We met at LaVarenne Cooking School, where we talked for an hour and a half before continuing our conversation outside on the streets of Paris. The following interview is adapted from "What's Cooking with Julia Child," published in the *Stars and Stripes*, European edition, September 27, 1984.

SHARON HUDGINS: To most people, you are famous as a cookbook author, cooking teacher, and television personality—but few people start out in life with the goal of writing cookbooks or starring on a television cooking show. When you were twenty years old, what did you want to be?

JULIA CHILD: A great novelist.

HUDGINS: Were you an English major?

CHILD: No, I wasn't. I decided when I went to Smith College in Northampton, Massachusetts, that as long as I was going to be a great novelist, I shouldn't take English. I should take other things like chemistry and history and so forth, so that's what I did. And then, of course, I never became a great novelist at all. I got a job in New York. I wanted to get into publishing, naturally, so I first tried the *New Yorker*, which had no interest in me whatsoever because I had nothing to contribute to them. And then I tried *Newsweek*. And I finally got a job at W. & J. Sloane's furniture store on Fifth Avenue doing public relations and advertising, which, as a matter of fact, was a very good introduction to publishing.

HUDGINS: What sort of work did you do during all those years before you finally became a food writer?

CHILD: Well, we had the war—World War II, that is—and I got into the OSS [Office of Strategic Services]. That took about four years or so. I was in Washington, DC, for about two years, and then they began sending people overseas, and I knew I'd sometime get to Europe, so I signed up to go to the Far East—and landed in Ceylon and in China, which was fascinating.

HUDGINS: What year was that?

CHILD: That was about 1942 or 1943. The OSS was a fascinating place to be in, because you had all those people who knew anything about the Far East—anthropologists, geographers, missionaries, all kinds of people. That's where I met my husband, Paul—in Ceylon. And after about a year and a half or so in Ceylon, he went up to China, and then I found out that I would have to go up there, too, which I did. I was never anything more than in the files section. I established the intelligence files in Ceylon, and then I had to do the same thing up in China, which was fascinating. I was awfully lucky to have been there then, because that was when you had Chiang Kai-shek, and then you had the Communist Chinese up in the north. Nobody really quite knew what they were—some people said they were "agrarian reformers." Had we had Barbara Tuchman's book on [General Joseph W.] Stilwell [*Stilwell and the American Experience in China, 1911–1945*], it would have helped everyone a great deal, because nobody knew General Stilwell very well, and he was very difficult—sort of a sourpuss of a man. My husband worked with him and liked him very much, but for most other people, he was impossible to get along with. And nobody knew what a marvelous background he had, that he really knew all about the Communists—exactly who they were and what they were up to. I think had he not been so difficult, the course of our [America's] Chinese career would have been different. Roosevelt was not interested at that point, and they had a fellow called Pat Hurley [President Franklin Roosevelt's personal representative to Generalissimo Chiang Kai-shek] who was sort of like a bull in a china shop. And I think we really messed things up in China from our lack of knowledge. But it was fascinating to be there.

HUDGINS: Where were you in China—and for how long?

CHILD: We were almost two years in China, first in Kunming, which was fascinating. It looked very much like California, with eucalyptus trees—a beautiful, beautiful town. And then I had to start a registry or file system up in Chongqing, so I had three or four months there. I was very lucky to have had that.

HUDGINS: When Chiang Kai-shek was there?

CHILD: Yes, Chiang Kai-shek was there. It was really before the internal civil war there. And then I went back down to Kunming again, and then we came out through India, after the Bomb dropped. We stayed about a month or so, and then some of our detachment of OSS was going on to Shanghai—and I decided that it was time that I went home. It's interesting to me that we were so ill prepared [for the war]. I've just been reading William Manchester's life of General MacArthur [*American Caesar: Douglas MacArthur, 1880–1964*]. In the Philippines, we had nothing. Of course, we thought these silly little yellow men were not to be taken seriously, and we could beat them before breakfast with our hands tied behind our backs. We had World War I guns, we had no airplanes, we had nothing. It was appalling to think how unprepared we were for the Philippines and how much we lost just through ignorance and damn foolishness. I think that if we allowed ourselves to get into such a state of unpreparedness again, we would probably have that much trouble. It's awfully hard to know what to do, but certainly we should never be in a situation like that. And we shouldn't overdo, either.

HUDGINS: What did you do next? After you left the Far East?

CHILD: Well, anyway, we had such a fascinating time. We met so many interesting people in the OSS—intellectuals, whom I'd really not had much to do with before. I was sort of a plain old middle-class *bourgeoise*. [*laughs*] I was not an intellectual type. And when we got back, that's when—well, Paul and I had known each other, and we decided we wouldn't do anything until we got back, because army life was so strange—we decided we ought to look at each other's families, and by that time, he was forty-two, and I was thirty-two, so we didn't have to rush into anything.

HUDGINS: So you were married after you got back from the Far East?

CHILD: We were married after we got back, and that was when he was transferred back into the United States Information Agency—actually it was part of the State Department then. Then we lived in Washington [DC], which was fun, for about two years, and then they began sending people abroad. And he had lived in France for a long time as a young man and spoke very good French, so we were sent over to the Paris embassy. We arrived the day that Truman was elected.

HUDGINS: So, 1948 is when you began your life in France? You finally got to Europe, as you knew all along you would.

CHILD: I finally got to Europe and was in hysterics for about three years because it was so marvelous there. The food was so marvelous, and I just loved the French and the French life.

HUDGINS: Was it here in France that you learned to cook, or had you already learned to cook before that?

CHILD: No, I had cooked a bit. I found that after I married,

I enjoyed cooking very much, but I didn't know much about it. I had *Gourmet* magazine and *Joy of Cooking.* After we got off the boat, we drove to Rouen, where I had my first French meal, and I've never turned back! It was so good! We had oysters and *sole meunière* and *crème fraîche* and beautiful wine.

HUDGINS: You remember that first French meal so vividly?

CHILD: I certainly do!

HUDGINS: What advice would you give to someone who is just learning to cook—to a real beginner?

CHILD: Either take some cooking lessons or cook with friends, which I think is one of the very best ways of doing things. Find a good friend who's also a good cook, and anytime that he or she has a dinner party, say that you'd like to come over and help. That's kind of like the French apprentice system. And get a good cookbook. There are a lot of good books around. Get one and follow it seriously and just start cooking. I think some people keep putting it off, and the thing to do is to start right in. Plunge in fearlessly! That's what I'm always saying. Be a fearless cook!

HUDGINS: What is it that makes a really good cook?

CHILD: Hunger. Greed. [*laughs*] And also just the enjoyment of working with your hands. If you like hand work, then cooking is wonderfully creative work, I think. It takes all of your intelligence and all of your dexterity. It's always creative, it's always new, it's always fun. I mean, unless you don't like to eat—and some people don't. And I see no excuse for people who say, "Oh, well, I work all day, and I just can't come home and fix anything nice." It's very easy to cook. You don't have to cook anything fancy, but just get good, fresh food. It can be very simple indeed.

HUDGINS: You use the terms *good food* and *good cooking* a lot, but there are some people who would say that a casserole containing Hamburger Helper, instant onion soup, and crushed potato chips is good food, meaning that they enjoy eating it. What are your own criteria for determining what *good food* is?

CHILD: First, I think you have to learn how to eat. It took me certainly a time, living here [in France], to learn how to eat, to learn what really good food tastes like. I think that's one reason why it's very important to come to France, where cooking is taken seriously, and to taste what the real thing is supposed to be like. But I think that in America, food is getting better and better—our standards are getting better. It's interesting that in France the pleasure of cooking is not a middle-class hobby the way it is in the United States. We know very few French people who enjoy cooking at all. It's just sort of not considered. Or somebody who's had university training does *not* go into food the way we do in the States now. Just think of this International Association of Cooking Schools. We have over nine hundred members from all over the country—and the world—most of whom are middle-class people with educations. It's very hard running this cooking school [LaVarenne] to find any French people who know about cooking who could be useful to them. It's very difficult. Cooking is not considered a serious discipline. What we're trying to do here with the IACS—and also with our new American Institute of Wine and Food—is to have professional cooking a real discipline, on a par with architecture, music, everything else.

HUDGINS: Then what accounts for such good cooking in France, in the home?

CHILD: I don't think you've got such good cooking in the homes anymore. Most people don't have hired help anymore, to do the cooking. I think often they [French housewives] can do a little bit, but they usually—when they're going to have anyone for dinner—they either take them out, or they go to the *charcuterie* and get something.

HUDGINS: So you're saying that the real traditions of French cooking exist on the professional level, in the restaurants, not in the homes.

CHILD: I would think so. And I think also the foreigners who come to the restaurants are far more critical of the food than the general French person is, because if you don't cook well yourself, you're not often a very good judge of what restaurant food is like—I mean, if you're used to bought charcuterie-type stuff. I think the French—who are very chauvinistic—would be horrified by that observation, but I think probably you get more careful analysis from foreigners than from French people.

HUDGINS: Your first cookbook, *Mastering the Art of French Cooking, Volume I,* was published in 1961. How did that come about?

CHILD: It was after we settled here that I got so interested in food and found that I wasn't going to be a great novelist— and found I'd been looking all my life for a profession. And I said, "This is it." So that's why I went to the Cordon Bleu cooking school. At that time—this was 1948, 1949—people, you know, sort of *bourgeois* people, were not going into cooking, and my friend Simone Beck, whom I hadn't met at that time, was doing the same thing.

HUDGINS: So you met her at the Cordon Bleu cooking school?

CHILD: No, I didn't meet her there, but we had some mutual friends in the embassy, and they knew that I was being this sort of weird person doing all of her own shopping and cooking, going to cooking school, and they had a friend called Simone—Simca—who was doing very much the same thing, and so they said, well, you ought to meet each other. And we both kind of fell into each other's arms. I had nobody to talk to who was interested in cooking. So it just worked out beautifully.

HUDGINS: And the first cookbook grew out of your association with Simone Beck?

CHILD: Yes, with Simca. She had been working with another French woman, Louisette Bertholle, who's written quite a few books on her own, and they had started a book on French cooking for Americans and were looking for an American collaborator, so it just worked out perfectly.

HUDGINS: What have you found to be the most difficult thing about writing a cookbook?

CHILD: It took us about eight years to get our first book out. Of course, we were learning as we were doing. I think you have to take it very seriously—that it's only as good as its worst recipe. If everything doesn't work, it's no good, so you just have to be really sure of what you're doing.

HUDGINS: So it took eight years to produce the first cookbook?

CHILD: Eight years for the first one. And then when we went back to the States, I got onto television. It was a very lucky thing in that there wasn't anyone else doing cooking on TV. And at that time, French cooking was very "in." With the Kennedys in the White House, people were very interested in it, so I had the field to myself, which was just damn lucky. It would be very, very—much more difficult now.

HUDGINS: You had *The French Chef* television series, which started in 1963. How many television shows have you done in all?

CHILD: Let's see, we did 119 black-and-whites, and I don't remember how many color we've done. We really did the whole gamut of French cooking. It's interesting to see the French television things [in France]—it just shows that the French women don't do anything. I mean, it's the most primitive, baby-type of cooking. And we, in our case [on American television], we've been through absolutely everything—the most complicated *homard à l'américaine, soufflé de Homard Plaza Athenée*, and all of the great French dishes. We've done practically everything.

HUDGINS: You've been on television for the last twenty years or so. What's been your most embarrassing moment on TV?

CHILD: Well, nothing much, because I think that in cooking you're so used to things going wrong anyway, and part of it is—if it goes wrong, you're not any good if you can't fix it up. I mean nothing particularly bothers me about it. People always ask me that, and I always say, "Everything always happens, and I'm tired of that question."

HUDGINS: I was going to ask what question you were tired of being asked—and now I know the answer. Actually, everybody knows that disasters occur in the kitchen, but perhaps you're a little famous for letting them show on television.

CHILD: But we don't *let* them show. The point is that if you have to stop, every single minute you're paying out hundreds of dollars, and unless it's something that's a real disaster— like when the oven caught on fire—you really can't afford to go back and fix it. At least you certainly can't with the budget we get on public television. You realize that it costs so much money, you'd better pick up and go on if you possibly can.

HUDGINS: There has been a greatly increased interest in food in the United States in the last fifteen to twenty years—

CHILD: Oh, tremendous, and really now showing in just the last few years. And in the last few years, a lot of educated people have gone into the business. It's considered a "proper profession" for you or any one of us to go into. There will be a lot more good foods—and people will concentrate on raising beautiful little vegetables, mushrooms, meat, or something like that.

HUDGINS: But at the same time, there has been a proliferation of packaged instant foods, frozen dinners, frozen "gourmet" dishes, etc.—in addition to all the fast-food eating places that have become so popular.

CHILD: Yes, but you always have to remember that we are a country of 230 million people, that if 5 million people are interested in good food—but obviously there are more than that, I mean, 20 million, let's say—that's an awful lot of people. So people keep talking about fast food, but there certainly is room for all of it. I certainly would much rather go to McDonald's and know exactly what I'm going to get than have lunch on an airplane or go to one of these bad restaurants. Because at least you know exactly what you're getting.

HUDGINS: What about American children, who seem to be interested merely in hot dogs, hamburgers, pizzas, etc.? I know we're generalizing again—

CHILD: I think you can never generalize. It depends very much on what the family gives them. I think everybody likes hot dogs and hamburgers and pizzas—I like them myself.

HUDGINS: I agree. But I've known children who don't want to eat anything but hamburgers, hot dogs, etc. They aren't interested in other foods. How do you go about broadening a child's culinary horizons?

CHILD: I think it's entirely up to the family. If the family are at all interested in food and health and adventure, then you take your children marketing and discuss, "Well, let's try that," and you take them out to restaurants, and you make food part of their education, part of the family fun. But if you're going to have a stupid mother who just doesn't want to do anything but dump some sort of awful frozen dinner on them, I think that's the family's fault.

HUDGINS: The number of people who are interested in food is certainly growing.

CHILD: Oh, immensely. And they're being very influential. There's a great interest in fresh food. It's amazing what's happened in supermarkets [in the United States]. We have our place down in the south of France, and very often I say, "Well, I'd just as soon go to the Star Market in Cambridge, Massachusetts, because these vegetables are not fresh." Everyone keeps saying, "Oh, the marvelous *matières premières* in France," but I don't find that so, particularly down in the south. If things are in season, they're fine—but you get just the same old rock-hard tomatoes and rock-hard peaches and so forth when they're out of season there, as you do anywhere else. And I've had chickens that tasted like fish. But I think we have very, very good food in the States, where we can get it in Boston. And we have even better food in Santa Barbara, where we are in the winter. But then, I find I'm rather chauvinistic.

HUDGINS: Perhaps with good reason.

CHILD: I think if you're interested in good food, unless you're in a deprived area, you can certainly find it in the United States. You have to look around, but you have to look around here in France, too, to find the right places to go to.

HUDGINS: Do you think that *nouvelle cuisine* is undermining traditional French cooking?

CHILD: I think nouvelle cuisine has been refreshing, because when we were here [in France] a long time ago you couldn't change anything at all. It was just absolutely rigid, too traditional. But I also think that more natural food is going to come back again, but in a different way. It will never be the same as it was because I think people are much more conscious of calories now. When we were first here, you didn't mind how much butter you put into something. So I think nouvelle cuisine has been needed—a refreshment of traditional French cooking.

HUDGINS: In our conversation earlier today, you mentioned living in the Bonn–Bad Godesberg area of Germany. All the other countries you've lived and traveled in, besides France and the United States—have they influenced your cooking and the way you eat?

CHILD: Oh, everything has. Germany did. And Norway. Of course, we loved Norway—all the fresh fish. I think having had a thorough French training, I think you absorb that. And I just sort of do my own thing now. That's what most people do anyway.

HUDGINS: In conclusion, I'd like to ask something about your husband. You credit him with introducing you to French food. Does he also cook?

CHILD: Well, he *could*, but he doesn't. He's guinea pig number one for *my* cooking. I wouldn't have done anything without him because he was always very encouraging. He's wonderfully helpful, when we're giving parties, washing dishes, setting the table. He's just a very nice, helpful man. We like to do things together, so that makes a lot of difference. That's very important.

JULIA CHILD

INTERVIEW WITH POLLY FROST
INTERVIEW
AUGUST 1989

Since her first PBS television appearance as the French Chef in 1963, Julia Child has played a major role in awakening Americans to the pleasures of eating well. Julia—as she is called by everyone who knows her—is famous for her height (she's six feet one) and heartiness (she's seventy-seven, but anyone half her age has trouble keeping up with her). In person, what is striking is her unflagging generosity and openness. She's fun, like a favorite aunt who will take you along on her adventures, dispensing great advice all the while.

Born Julia McWilliams, she grew up in Pasadena, a suburb of Los Angeles, and went to boarding school outside San Francisco. After attending Smith College, she was a file clerk during World War II for the OSS in Burma and China, where she met her husband, Paul. After marrying, they lived in Paris, where he worked in the foreign service until 1954 and she took up serious cooking, studying at the Cordon Bleu. With Simone Beck, who has remained a close friend, she wrote two influential and popular cookbooks, *Mastering the Art of French Cooking*, volumes I and II (they had help on the first volume from Louisette Bertholle). Her new book, *The Way to Cook* (Knopf), includes classic techniques along with recipes for such dishes as hominy and moussaka. It should become a standard for both the advanced cook and the career person with limited time. Nowadays, she and her husband divide the year between Santa Barbara and Cambridge, Massachusetts. Julia always seems to be in motion. We met at eight o'clock on a summer morning at the Santa Barbara farmers' market. As we marveled at the bins of vegetables, fish, and flowers, people regularly approached her to say how much they liked her television show and to see what she was buying. "What do you do with this?" she asked one seller. "That's bitter melon. Chop it up and sauté with garlic and onions . . . I can't believe I'm telling you how to do this!" A man nearby said, "If we see this on TV next week—" "You'll know where I got it!" Julia called back. On our way to the car, a couple ran up to her with a book. "It's not one of yours, but it would mean so much if you'd sign it." "What book was it?" I asked her afterward. "Barbara Kafka's *Microwave Gourmet*," she laughed.

At midday, we drove an hour up the coast and cut inland to a winery, where Julia was one of the judges in a *bouilla-baisse* cook-off between Santa Barbara restaurants. There was every conceivable kind of fish stew in the running. "We had to give up our notions of what a bouillabaisse was and just go for taste," she said. After lunch I suggested that a siesta under the trees was in order—all this tasting and comparing was hard work. "I'd have to be made of pretty weak stuff to be exhausted by a bouillabaisse festival," Julia said, and we were off, back to her house to prepare some lamb and eggplant to take to a friend's for dinner. ("I'm not wild about those twenty-four-hour marinades," she said. "I like the flavors of the lamb to come through.")

The next day, we sampled some restaurants and visited with their chefs, then spent the afternoon attending meetings of local food and wine groups. At dinnertime, she gave me a lesson in how to cook omelettes. "Put the eggs in the pan, let them sit for a few seconds, then shake the pan so you spread the egg around. Then jerk it toward you—jerk, jerk, jerk. That makes it roll over on itself." I had read that Merce Cunningham admires Julia's movements, and they are certainly quick and precise, with no wasted motion.

"Let's sit down and eat these for dinner," she said when I'd produced two omelettes. "You're kidding," I said. I felt as though Fred Astaire had just asked me to dance. I was catching on to the shaking and jerking movements, but my omelettes still looked as if they'd come from the local diner. "You really don't have to…"

"No, no, no," she said. "This is how you learn." So we sat down at her dining table, which looks out over the Pacific Ocean, poured some wine, and ate and talked.

POLLY FROST: I'd love to be able to crack two eggs at the same time, the way you do.

JULIA CHILD: I saw that in the movies. It was that cute, dark-haired girl—

FROST: Oh, Audrey Hepburn, in *Sabrina*. She went to Paris and studied at the Cordon Bleu and then came back and made an omelette by cracking both eggs on the bowl. I was very impressed by that.

CHILD: So was I. I figured if she could do it, I could too.

FROST: I always forget, though: Did she marry William Holden or Humphrey Bogart?

CHILD: Well, somebody. But now, when you go home and make an omelette, remember: if you get nervous, just sit back and think about it, and then plunge in and do it again. It was Chef Bugnard who taught me how to make an omelette at the Cordon Bleu. He also taught me how to make scrambled eggs. I thought I knew how, but I didn't. Not the French way, which isn't flaky, but rather like a custard. When I got to France I realized I didn't know very much about food at all. I'd never had a real cake. I'd had those cakes from cake mixes or the ones that have a lot of baking powder in them. A really good French cake doesn't have anything like that in it—it's all egg power.

FROST: How did your family come to settle in Pasadena?

CHILD: As a young man, my grandfather came out in a covered wagon with his cousins. They thought he was frail, so they packed his shroud in his duffel bag. But he made it. He went back East and fought in the Civil War, then settled again on the family farm in Illinois. When he was sixty-five he moved out to California, and on the way he saw some nice-looking land in Arkansas for twenty-five cents an acre and turned it into a rice farm. He lived to be ninety-three. My father was in charge of managing the farm. But my mother came from New England, and she didn't think much of Arkansas, so they came out to Pasadena. My father was in real estate, banking, and land management. As family life, it was very conventional, happy, and comfortable. We weren't wealthy, but we were well-off.

FROST: What kind of woman was your mother?

CHILD: My mother was independent. She had grown up in Dalton and Pittsfield, in western Massachusetts, and she was one of the first women drivers in that area. I had a mean aunt who used to say, "Julia McWilliams, you read more books than anyone—and know less." Which hurt my mother—she thought that everything we did was wonderful. If we got a C–, she'd say, "Good, maybe next time you'll get a C."

FROST: Do you have any childhood memories of food?

CHILD: When I was a senior at Katharine Branson School in Ross, we were allowed to go over to San Francisco—we were able to go alone. We'd put on our cloche hats and take the ferry across. We'd stop in the city of Perris and buy lipstick. There was very nice restaurant in an alley, where nice young ladies went, and we would have cinnamon toast with lots and lots of butter on it and beautiful California artichokes with hollandaise sauce.

FROST: That's an amazing combination.

CHILD: When I was sent off to camp here in Santa Barbara, we all had to wear middy blouses, ties, and bloomers. We used to bead Indian headbands—the terrible thing was that after making them, we wore them. But the two women who ran the camp were wonderful cooks, and every Sunday they'd make these delicious pancakes, and we'd have a race to see who could eat the most.

FROST: How did you start out, after Smith?

CHILD: I graduated in '34. In my generation, except for a few people who'd gone into banking or nursing or something like that, middle-class women didn't have careers. You were to marry and have children and be a nice mother. You didn't go out and do anything. I found that I got restless a year or two after going home to Pasadena.

FROST: Were you always independent, or was that something you had to achieve?

CHILD: I must have always been independent because that kind of life, I just couldn't do. It didn't fulfill anything. So I moved to New York and lived with two roommates on East Fifty-Ninth Street near the bridge. Our rent was eighty dollars a month. I took a secretarial course, hoping to get a job at the *New Yorker*, and ended up at W. & J. Sloan furniture store working publicity. I loved it. I started out at eighteen dollars a week, and eventually I made twenty-two dollars a week. I remember lunch across the street from Sloan's was fifty cents. When the war broke out, I decided I would be very patriotic. Standing my full height, I presented myself to the WAC and the to the WAVES. And I was rejected—I was an inch too tall.

FROST: But you went to work for the OSS in Ceylon. What was that like?

CHILD: It was a beautiful country, full of ruined temples, caves with paintings, and water buffalo and grasses. And then, when the OSS opened an attachment in China—Kunming and Chongqing—I volunteered to go with them in the files section.

FROST: Your future husband was stationed there, too, wasn't he?

CHILD: Yes. Paul was in what was called presentation division, which made maps and diagrams. He was sent for because he was a very skillful mapmaker.

FROST: What kinds of women were over there with you?

CHILD: We had one or two upper-class intellectuals, but the rest of us were office help—secretaries, filing clerks. This was before women's liberation.

FROST: After the war, you and Paul went to Paris.

CHILD: We had a wonderful apartment right across form the Concorde bridge on the third floor of an old private house. Paris in those days was simple and nice. We'd park our big Buick right outside the house. The food was marvelous— old-fashioned, classical French food.

FROST: That's where you took up serious cooking.

CHILD: Yes. I wanted something that would hold me and sustain me. Cooking was taken with such seriousness in France that even ordinary chefs were proud of their profession. That's what appealed to me.

FROST: When you came back to America you became friends with James Beard.

CHILD: After *Mastering the Art of French Cooking*—the first book Simone Beck and I wrote, with Louisette Bertholle—came out, our editor said, "Whom would you like to meet?" Simone said Dione Lucas, and I said James Beard. So we went down to where he was teaching on Tenth Street. He was actually teaching a class when we arrived, and he welcomed us in. The students were all covered with egg white! He loved to have them fold the soufflé with their hands. He said to them, "Look at this beautiful big book," and showed it to the whole class. He took us to lunch the next day at the Four Seasons. That was our beginning with Jim. He was a big, huggable man, about six feet four. He used to visit us in our house in France.

FROST: Who was Dione Lucas?

CHILD: You don't know who she was? She was one of the very first people who brought French cooking to America, a wonderful technician. She had the Egg Basket restaurant by Bloomingdale's. She was one of the first television cooks, and she had a famous cooking school. A lot of people adored her. She was tremendously talented and worked like a dog, but money just slipped through her fingers.

FROST: You and James Beard must have cooked some great meals?

CHILD: We cooked together a lot. Once we followed Madam Saint-Agnes's way of doing *cèpe* mushrooms. You chop the stems up very fine and sauté them like regular mushrooms, with garlic and parsley, and then you cut the caps very evenly, not too thin, and cook them very slowly in fresh olive oil. Very, very slowly, so that they're beautifully tender inside and just beginning to get crisp outside.

FROST: Mmm. Did the two of you ever argue over cooking?

CHILD: No, because we'd do our own thing, or we'd try something we'd never done before. We did a joint demonstration once. I did a New England clam chowder and he did a Manhattan one. It was on one of those winter days when it was supposed to be cold, but of course it warmed up. We made the New England chowder and mistakenly put in bread crumbs, which began to ferment. When we took the soup out to show the crowd, it was seething. Seething! So we had to throw it away and start over.

FROST: Fans have come up to you every time we've been out together. But you seem to handle it very well. It would be terrible to be a celebrity who couldn't go out, like Elvis.

CHILD: [*laughs*] That's different. That was based on sex, and my fame is based on one of life's necessities. And you know that as soon as you're off the tube, people will forget all about you.

FROST: Do you get many angry letters from people about your television show?

CHILD: Not really, but once in a while I get a letter from a vegetarian. I have a letter somewhere in my files from the widow of Nathan Pritikin. That whole operation has been a gold mine. She said that she had seen me slathering butter around on my program, so I gave her my usual talk about moderation in all things. Even Pritikin could have used a little nice food once in a while. Following his diet might prolong your life three or four days, but it wouldn't be worth it.

FROST: How do you shop?

CHILD: I always try to buy just what I need. You get ideas as to what's in season and what's best. I think if you have a preconceived idea before shopping, that makes it difficult. You have to have an open mind.

FROST: A lot of people go out shopping with a recipe and buy what it tells them to.

CHILD: That's the wrong thing to do. You learn to cook so that you don't have to be a slave to recipes. You get what's in season and you know what to do with it.

FROST: What are your favorite vegetables?

CHILD: I love root vegetables: carrots, parsnips, and turnips. Now that's something, with a lot of taste—turnips. I'm a beet freak. I put them in the pressure cooker. Have you tried that? They're so easy—fifteen minutes and they're done.

FROST: How about some tips on how to buy produce?

CHILD: If you're buying tomatoes, for example, pick them up and smell them—they should have a lovely perfume. They need to be kept at fifty degrees or above, particularly during the growing season, because that's when they develop their flavor. Like most things we eat, if they're really going to be good, you have to pay them a lot of attention. But I'd be willing to pay practically a dollar for one that had a good perfume to it.

FROST: I find one of the hardest things about cooking is that so many of my friends have eating obsessions. One won't eat any cholesterol, another's hypoglycemic, another's a vegetarian . . . Of course, some people have genuine health problems, which I'm sympathetic to, but—

CHILD: But not very many. I think it's more that people are afraid. A lot of it is just misinformation and general scare tactics that the press uses to make a good story. I think one of the terrible things today is that people have this deathly fear of food: fear of eggs, say, or fear of butter. Most doctors feel that you can have a little bit of everything.

FROST: What concerns about food do you consider legitimate?

CHILD: I'm very much for making everything safe. The more natural the means we use to raise our vegetables and get rid of bugs, the better. But it can be quite expensive. In this country, we have 260 million people to feed, and I think we're handling this remarkably well, but we have to do serious studies. And this administration seems to me much more interested in protecting big business and money today than in thinking of the future.

FROST: Is eating shellfish too dangerous a thing to do right now?

CHILD: The shellfish thing is very scary. You have to know the people you buy from and exactly where their wholesalers are getting the fish from. Legal Seafood's, in Boston, has its own laboratory so it can test for bacterial content.

FROST: What do you think of the rise of the animal-rights movement?

CHILD: We've gotten very emotional, considering animals as people. Animals that we eat are raised for food in the most economical way possible, and the serious food producers do it in the most humane way possible. I think anyone who is a carnivore needs to understand that meat does not originally come in these neat little packages. If you go to a chicken place, you'll see how they're raised and how they're picked up in the dead of night and carried to the slaughterhouse and hung there. Their throats are cut, and they're bled. Then they go through a machine with rubber paddles, and then they go through another place where a big machine goes *shoosh!* and sucks out their guts, and so forth. We always think it's wonderful that we can get chickens so inexpensively. Well, that's how you mass-produce chicken.

FROST: Some people would say that's a reason not to eat chicken.

CHILD: Then they shouldn't eat chicken. But I don't think it's fair for one group to forbid another group to eat the kind of food they like to eat. People liked to eat veal until they saw pictures of these darling little animals with brown eyes. Veal calves have been raised the same way for centuries. If it's going to be real prime veal, the calves have to be raised in confinement; they cannot run around. Some people feel that if you're going to cook a lobster it's more humane to get a kettle of cold water and bring it slowly to a boil. That's actually one of the most cruel things to do, because the lobster suffocates to death. It's far better to plunge it headfirst into boiling water. Or you could take a knife and cut through the eyes. But if you're going to go into all that, I think you ought to give up and let somebody else do it.

FROST: Do free-range chickens have a happier life?

CHILD: It depends on what's meant by *free-range*. Haven't you seen some of these free-range chickens in tiny little pens walking around in their excrement?

FROST: Do you consider yourself more of a teacher, a performer, or a cook?

CHILD: I love to teach—that's my role. Teaching should never be dull, even if you're talking about how to raise turnips in Denmark. Cooking hasn't yet been accepted as the art form it is. It should be on the level with any of the other art forms. You can get a degree in fine arts–dance. I'd like for people to be able to go to the universities and get a degree in fine arts–gastronomy. What's needed are people who can be leaders in the profession, which they can't be without an education. You need to be very well educated in languages and history and art. You need aesthetics, as well as chemistry and other things. Many culinary schools aren't doing what they ought to. It's wrong to suggest to students that they're chefs after two years. What I like about the field is that when you get into it, it really becomes a passionate interest. It can involve you totally.

FROST: I know you have strong political convictions. Having worked in television so much, what do you think about the way the "moral" right uses the medium?

CHILD: I was in Memphis doing a cooking demonstration for Planned Parenthood—I'm tremendously involved with Planned Parenthood—and there was a very small group of right-to-lifers there. Every time they appeared they'd have little babies in their arms with signs saying IF YOU HAD YOUR WAY I WOULDN'T HAVE BEEN BORN. There were only ten in all, but every time they appeared, they'd be photographed by television. Just because they were there, it was news; we who are pro women's rights must do a great deal to get our views across.

FROST: What do you think of the current political climate in general?

CHILD: I don't think this administration seems interested in doing anything about the environment. These people are anti-abortion, but they're not doing anything for the future. If we go on as we are, polluting everything, we may very well end up like Venus, a great ball of fire. And I don't think we have very much time. Our president also supports the National Rifle Association. What possible reason does anyone have to own an attack rifle? I don't think there's any reason for anyone to own a gun that isn't registered. Paul and I were over in Europe during the McCarthy era. Because we'd been in the OSS, we knew a number of people who'd been attacked by the McCarthyites. Their lives and careers were ruined. People were hysterical about Communism the way people today are hysterical about flag burning. I'm really against these people who try to show that they're great patriots, because they're not thinking, they're just being hysterical.

FROST: Pasadena, where you grew up, isn't a place that's known for its food or its liberal views.

CHILD: I was kind of an innocent hayseed from a middle-class, utterly nonintellectual background. Then during the war, I suddenly met all these fascinating intellectuals. And Paul, a sophisticated man, knew about art and had lived in France. One thing he has taught me is the scientific approach. I think my training in cooking has helped a great deal, but mostly it was Paul. I was a romantic, messy thinker. I was raised with very conservative beliefs, but that was a long time ago. In between I've lived in a lot of places, which makes a big difference. After a while you decide that you can have your own opinions.

"WE KNEW A LOT OF FAIRLY IMPORTANT PEOPLE AT THAT POINT"

INTERVIEW WITH JEWELL FENZI
THE FOREIGN AFFAIRS ORAL HISTORY PROJECT,
FOREIGN SERVICE SPOUSE SERIES
NOVEMBER 7, 1991

JEWELL FENZI: This is Jewell Fenzi on Thursday, November 7, 1991. I am interviewing Julia Child at my home. Julia Child has come to Washington for a promotion of her latest book, *The Way to Cook*, and has kindly agreed to share an hour of her time with me this morning.

JULIA CHILD: When I was in the Foreign Service, they didn't really pay attention to wives at all. A lot of them never learned the language, or did anything.

FENZI: And that was 1944?

CHILD: We [Child and her husband, Paul] were in World War II, we were in the OSS and we met in Ceylon, or Sri Lanka—it was Ceylon then. Then we went up to China, and we were there when the bomb dropped. Then we came back to Washington, and Paul's OSS Department—they called it visual presentation, maps, diagrams, war rooms, and things like that—became the US Information Agency.

So we were there in Washington. Paul had spent a lot of his young manhood in France and spoke beautiful French, really practically bilingual. When they were setting up the

USIS [United States Information Service] in Paris, he was asked to go over, which was, of course, wonderful for us. Outside of the Far East, I had only been to Tijuana.

And I had had French all of my life, but when I got over there, I could neither speak it nor understand it. So I went to Berlitz two hours every day. And then we had some friends from New Haven who were medieval art historians, and they introduced us to their colleagues in France. They were called the Group Focillon, and there was Henri Focillon, who was the great medievalist, and his son-in-law was a Lithuanian, Jurgis Baltrušaitis, and his wife, Hélène, was the stepdaughter of Focillon and her mother, who was known as Tante Guiguitte, was partially American—I am not quite sure. Anyway, we met Hélène because Jurgis, at that point, was giving some lectures in the States for about six months, and Hélène became really my best friend. We said that we would meet every Monday for an exchange of lessons, but of course it turned out to be entirely French. They had medieval Wednesday evenings, and Paul and I always went to them, and everything was in French, which was good. There would be long, long discussions about whether the false transepts had been built in 1123 or 1131, and things like that.

But that was wonderful just to be drowned in French. And then, I had never had French food before. I loved the Chinese food, it was just delicious. And I just fell in love with French food from the first bite. We came over I think it was on the SS *America* with our old blue Buick, and our first French meal, or my French meal, was in Rouen, and I never, never turned back after that. After we had gotten settled*, I enrolled in the Cordon Bleu and I was fortunately able to join a group of GIs on the Bill of Rights and we had a wonderful old chef [Max Bugnard] who had trained under Escoffier and was a real classicist and a wonderful man. We would start at seven in the morning and cook until about eleven. Then I would rush home and cook Paul a fancy lunch and go back again. I think it was the Cordon Bleu that helped me a great deal also because that was all in French.

FENZI: And you were the only woman in the class?

CHILD: I was the only woman in that class with the men. I just became passionate, I had been looking for a career all my life. I wanted to be on the *New Yorker* or something like that. Well, this was it. I was passionately interested in it, the tremendous care that all the chefs and teachers took. It was art for art's sake. It made no difference how long it took. If it came out beautifully, that was it. That was very appealing. After I had been to the Cordon Bleu, heavens, [after] about six or eight months, it began repeating. You can just do a chaudfroid. Well, about the third time you feel that, you have had it.

Luckily at that time I had met my French colleague, Simone Beck. Of course that was '48–'49, and all of the Americans [in France] could hire servants for practically nothing. And the French bourgeoisie all had their little

---

*   The Childs rented "a comfortable third-floor apartment on the Rue de l'Université behind the Chambre de Députés. Paul could walk across the Pont de la Concorde to his office . . . " (*The New Yorker*, December 23, 1974).

femmes de ménage, and I was so enthusiastic about this profession, but there wasn't anyone to talk to of my own type. We had mutual friends who introduced me to Simca, as she was known, and Jean at a cocktail party, and we literally embraced each other immediately because she felt the same way about, "Whom can I talk to!" She had a colleague, Louisette Bertholle, and the two of them were working together on a book on French cooking for Americans. They had a collaborator who died. I was delighted with that. That was after we had started our little cooking school. We had some American friends who knew what I was doing, and they said, "Well, we don't speak any French, so why don't you teach us?"

I felt that I didn't know nearly enough. But Simca, who had been cooking all of her life, and had worked with Henri Pellaprat [an instructor at Cordon Bleu] and so forth, said, "Well, why not?" So we started our cooking school about the next day and we called it the L'École des Trois Gourmandes, the School of the Three Hearty Eaters. That really started us seriously. Then their collaborator died, and that pleased me very much. I never knew him. Good timing. So we started in on our book together, and that took a long gestation period. It wasn't done until our last post in Norway, which was in '59.

FENZI: I think it's extraordinary that you carried that on via correspondence for how many years?

CHILD: Yes, but we kept meeting each other all the time.

FENZI: Well, you weren't really too far away in Marseille, Bonn, and Oslo.

CHILD: No, and Simca came down and visited us [in Marseille]. And you can do so much by correspondence, anyway.

FENZI: This was before the days of fax.

CHILD: Yes, it certainly was. And computers. And when I think that I would make six copies on my old standard typewriter. Then correcting those six copies. It was terrible. Just awful.

FENZI: It's the type of thing you can't believe you did.

CHILD: Well, but everybody did it. And when I think of living here in Washington with no air conditioning. It was horrible, but that was the way everybody lived. So that's my career. [*Pauses*] It was very nice having a hobby and profession at the same time because you met all kinds of people, and it was a very good introduction to the French as well. And I gave cooking lessons.

I guess I didn't do any in Germany, but when we got to Oslo, there was an American Women's Club and I remember the first luncheon I went to, which would have been in probably '59. It was a typical ladies' luncheon. They had a salad made out of Jell-O, I guess, and it had bananas and grapes and marshmallows and it was shaped . . . and really it looked like a phallic symbol. It was sitting on a little piece of lettuce, you couldn't hide it under anything. Then it [the luncheon] ended with one of those cake-mix cakes with a white mountain of coconut frosting. Horrible! And some of us got together and said, "Never again!" So we had a cooking committee so we couldn't end up with anything like that again.

I gave cooking lessons there in Norway with a mixed . . . Norway was an awfully nice post. Oslo, we just loved it. So many nice people, and then, of course, they all spoke English. Even though you were learning Norwegian, so it was very easy to get along with them, and they are such nice people anyway. So we loved our last post. After Norway, Paul had said that when he was sixty, he was going to retire because he never really liked the bureaucracy at all. And so we left when he was sixty, and that's when my book [*Mastering the Art of French Cooking*] came out. And he helped me with all of that. He helped me with proofreading and the index. He's a wonderful photographer, so he did photographs from which we had a sketch artist do drawings. So it was wonderful having him.

FENZI: He was very supportive, wasn't he?

CHILD: Oh, very, in everything. He was a prime dishwasher and baggage carrier. And then he was good intellectually for me, for I was rather messy intellectually. But he would always talk about the operational proof, and things like that. We had a very good time together.

FENZI: I guess I am just a half generation later, and, you see, it never occurred to me before *Mastering the Art* came out that there was not a step-by-step French cookbook. So, what was your jumping off point? You had to go and observe the chefs at the Cordon Bleu and then make notes, or what?

CHILD: No, I think you learn an awful lot from teaching, because at that point I had had the classical background. I was always learning. And we also had our wonderful . . . the man on the back [of *Mastering the Art*], chef Max Bugnard. He came and taught at our school, and also another wonderful one, a pastry chef, [Claude] Thillmont, and he would come and teach. And then there was a man who was very good at demonstrating, Pierre Mangelatte, and he also was chef at a wonderful little restaurant up in Montmartre. The wonderful thing about that profession is that you are always learning. I remember talking to an old chef, even Bugnard, who said, "Just about every day I learn something new." It's a very wonderfully creative profession.

FENZI: And also to be able to go from your lessons to all of the delightful little restaurants around Paris.

CHILD: Yes, and what was wonderful—those were the days of the classic cuisine, and it was so good. It was delicious. Just a plain roast chicken was so good. That was before they had learned to do battery-raised chicken. They really tasted like chicken. And delicious vegetables and salads and cheeses and so forth.

FENZI: While you were learning at class, you must have gone to little restaurants.

CHILD: Oh, in the old days, I think Paul's salary was six thousand dollars, and I got one hundred dollars a month from my family. But we had envelopes, and we each had two dollars a week allowance, and we had everything budgeted out, and we very carefully saved everything for going out. But even so, we could go out two or three times a week, and even a great restaurant like the Grand Véfour was only about three-fifty Or was it ten. I think maybe it was ten dollars. But you could eat beautifully for a reasonable price. But we had to watch every penny.

FENZI: I am also interested in the McCarthy era. Because you were in Paris.

CHILD: When it broke, we were in Marseille. During the McCarthy thing we were in Marseille, and when [Roy] Cohn and [David] Schine came through, I think we were still there.* We went up to Paris shortly afterward, and I remember our cultural attaché, Larry Morris—he was an older man, I guess he was in his fifties. They [Cohn and Schine] had arrived in Paris, and, of course, they went out to all the nightclubs and so forth, and it happened to be during Easter, and on Easter Sunday they had called a meeting that everyone was to get there at eight o'clock a.m. at the USIS office.

Of course, they didn't appear. It turned out that when they finally got hold of them, they were sleeping off a night at Montmartre. They had ruined everyone's weekend. I remember they were charging though the USIS, and Larry Morris came in and saw Cohn sitting at his desk with his feet on his desk. Larry Morris said, "Get out of that chair.

---

*   Reference to infamous European trip made by McCarthy's two bullying
      assistants.

Get your feet off my desk." But most people were scared to do anything. They were also the kind of people that if you really came at them, they would back right off. But most people didn't dare.

I remember Allen Dulles [Director of the Central Intelligence Agency at the time], as I was told, when they wanted to investigate the CIA, he said, "If you are going to investigate anyone, you can investigate me." They never touched him. But if you cringed, they were right on top of you. I never met them myself. There were also the people who just cravenly fell down in front of them. And we had quite a number of people who were just ruined by them. John Carter Vincent [Minister to Switzerland from 1947 to 1951] was one of the noted Chinese specialists drummed out of the Foreign Service by McCarthy's tactics. Vincent and others were accused of losing China to the Chinese communists led by Mao Zedong. He [Vincent] was a good friend of ours. He was drummed out. I remember we were back in Paris—I guess when were stationed in Marseille—John Carter Vincent came over and gave a talk at the American Club, and he had a standing ovation. It was horrible what they did to him.

FENZI: I was just reading Caroline Service's* transcript [of her interview] done at Berkeley, and, of course, he was treated very shabbily.

---

* Wife of John Stewart Service, also a Chinese specialist, or "China Hand," forced out of the Foreign Service by Senator McCarthy. He was reinstated after six years of legal negotiations.

CHILD: Jack Service, yes. They were all our era.

FENZI: I was interested in her transcript also because the first place she went in the Foreign Service was Kunming. And I was reading about Kunming.

CHILD: Because we were there.

FENZI: Yes. She first went about ten years before you did, and she said it was dirty and isolated, and she was homesick.

CHILD: It was beautiful—it looked like California.

FENZI: But I imagine that going as an OSS officer and being in charge—you were in charge.

CHILD: Paul was in charge of this visual presentation. I was always in the files, but at least I knew what was going on. I had no qualifications whatsoever, because during the war I had no languages. I could type, I had gotten my first job. I was still studying shorthand. I got to "It was a gray day when Ted ran the great race," and I never got further than that. It would have been useful. So I had no qualifications of any sort.

I started out [in Washington] at a place called Mellett's Madhouse, which was across from the Willard Hotel. There was a nasty little woman, a little naval officer with feet that went like that [*does a staccato tap, tap, tap with her fingers*]. She was in charge, but horrid, you know. She never gave you a smile. I was typing little white cards, and I was so furious at my job that I typed them so hard that they had to get two people to replace me when I left. I thought I should get a job by myself without any pull, and that's what I landed—I had friends in the OSS—so I applied for that, and I ended up in General Donovan's [director of the OSS's] file room, and he was a fascinating man. Kind of smallish and rumpled, piercing blue eyes, and it was said that he could read by just turning the pages. He was one of those people who could take the whole thing in. I don't know what there was about him, but people were just wonderfully loyal to him. I think that he took people very personally, was interested in them. So I was in his files, and then they started an air-sea-rescue equipment section, and I moved over to that, and I was administrative assistant; that's the only time I really got out of the files. I had to order them being made. And then they started sending people overseas, and I knew that I would eventually get to France, so I applied to the Far East. And thank heaven I did.

FENZI: Did you come to Mellett's Madhouse as a recruit in the Foreign Service auxiliary?

CHILD: Oh, no, this had nothing to do with the Foreign Service. I just came in as a plain person. And just to be sure that I wasn't being disloyal to my country, I applied to both the WAC and the WAVES, standing to my full height, and I was an inch and a half too long. Thank heavens, so I didn't have to go in there, which I wouldn't have liked. But I did apply, so I was patriotic. Luckily, I was tall. So Mellett's Madhouse I got all by myself. It just shows what you can do without any pull. And no talents.

But it was fascinating being with Donovan. I saw everybody, and I knew who they were. And then our first post was Ceylon. We were in Kandy, Ceylon, and we had a fascinating and amusing girl, Jane Foster, who came from San Francisco. She was terribly funny, kind of scatterbrained and very funny, and all kinds of ridiculous things would happen to her. Everyone adored her because she was just so amusing. Then when we were on post in Paris, we had a friend who came through and said that he had heard that Jane Foster was somewhere in Paris and he just wondered where she was. And so several people wondered about that, and one day we were walking along the quay, and we saw a poster, she was an artist, saying PAINTINGS BY JANE FOSTER. So we hied ourselves to the gallery and left a note, and when we got home, we had a call from Jane, and she was indeed in Paris, and she had married a rather short, funny little fellow, who I think was . . . I don't know what nationality he was. But she was as funny as ever, and we were stationed at Marseille at that point, and every time we would come up to Paris, we would see them.

And then, when we were in Germany, Paul suddenly got a call—no, there was a cable—and it said SEND CHILD AT ONCE TO WASHINGTON. I said I know why he is going; they are going to make him head of the department. Well, he got back there, and it turned out it was an FBI examination. And the first thing they said to him was, "Are you a homosexual?" He was furious. He said to the agent, "Take down your pants! How could you tell anything [that way]?" It was something like that. He was absolutely furious. He thought it was horrible. But I think they often do that so if you are homosexual, you often admit it. They dropped the homosexual bit and went on to question him about colleagues, friends, etc., etc. We knew a lot of fairly important people at that point. As soon as he got out that first day, he went howling to everybody he knew and, after a while, another day or two of investigation, it turned out it was all about Jane Foster, who had turned out to be a Russian agent. I think this chap she was married to was Russian. So they sent Paul back by way of Brussels to help pick out the site for the [1958 World's] Fair.

FENZI: I don't think they are bothered about that so much anymore.

CHILD: I should think they would. I have no idea. But it was a horrible experience for him. Then, of course, McCarthy turned out to be a homosexual and so did Cohn. And Cohn died of AIDS. Yes, a dreadful man. We had some English friends, and all of our English friends were absolutely horrified by the McCarthy thing. They thought it was just like the beginning of Nazi Germany.

FENZI: Did you hear the references to McCarthyism during the Thomas hearings?

CHILD: Well, I heard as much as I could. Those were disgusting, dreadful. Dreadful. Well, we were always down around rank four, so we didn't have to do any embassy things. We had our French friends, and we lived a very, very nice life. We had no really diplomatic responsibilities, and Jefferson

Caffery was ambassador when we were there.* He was an old line, kind of a strange fellow, when you would go through a reception line, he and his wife would sort of push you on like that. Shaking hands then . . . [*gesture of dismissal*]. And then Dillon was ambassador, he and his wife were charming, and then the Bohlens were there, and we had already known them anyway. They were charming people.

FENZI: Their daughter has gone back now as deputy chief of mission.

CHILD: That's what I hear. We are good friends with Anne Willan, who runs the LaVarenne cooking school, and I think they are great friends of young Avis . . . or Celestine. Of course, she is not so young anymore, is she? And then they had a son—I wonder what's happened to him, I wonder.

FENZI: I don't know about a son. I called Avis Bohlen's home here the other day because one of her mother's friends, Fanny Chipman, came up from Florida to receive the transcript [of her interview] at our annual benefit tea last week. Mrs. [Susan] Baker [wife of Secretary of State James A. Baker III] presents the transcripts, and Mrs. Chipman wanted Avis to come since the Chipmans and the Bohlens had been in Moscow together. This is one of the changes in the Foreign Service that we are documenting with these interviews. Avis Bohlen was the prototype Foreign Service wife of the 1960s.

---

* Jefferson Caffery was ambassador to France from 1944 to 1949; C. Douglas Dillon from 1953 to 1957; and Charles E. Bohlen from 1962 to 1968.

CHILD: Mother Avis.

FENZI: Yes. And, of course, she was a tremendous support system to Chip Bohlen in Moscow, in Paris, and in Manila. And so now the daughter is going back, not as a support for a male officer, but is the officer herself.

CHILD: Is she married?

FENZI: Yes, and his name is Calleo. He will be staying here in Washington, I believe, so the question is, who is filling that role for Avis Bohlen Jr., that her mother filled for her father. This is one of the changes in the service. I'm not saying that it's bad, but you wonder if maybe diplomacy . . .

CHILD: Well, when we were at our last post in Norway, we had a woman, Frances Willis, of whom we were all very, very fond.* And she had an old mother living with her, but she had to do all that herself.

FENZI: Yes. Well, now, she would get an allowance, which would permit her to hire a housekeeper to do that for her.

CHILD: I also remember when we were in Marseille, we had the first black—he didn't look black, he looked like a

---

* Frances Willis was the first female career Foreign Service officer to receive an ambassadorial appointment. She was named ambassador to Switzerland (1953–57) by Harry S. Truman, and later served as ambassador to Norway (1957–61) and to Ceylon (1961–64).

Portuguese—Cliff Wharton, and his wife, Leonie, and she was wonderfully supportive. She was a darling woman. And before that, we had had a chap who was called Hayward Hill, who we all called Hill the Pill. He was really uncomfortable in his skin. He always wore gray gloves and a homburg, even in Marseille. He didn't like the house that was provided, so sometimes he would sleep in his office and sometimes at a hotel. So when Cliff Wharton arrived, there was no house for him. But it was interesting, everybody sort of hated each other [when Hill was there]. But when Cliff Wharton arrived, within an hour, things had changed.

FENZI: Morale comes from the top.

CHILD: Yes, in Marseille when we had Cliff, it was wonderful. Let's see, whom did we have in Germany? Conant, who came after Conant? Germany was a great big post.

FENZI: I remember reading somewhere that you took a stove—a big restaurant stove—from France to Germany.

CHILD: Well, that's untrue.

FENZI: Well, thank heavens. All I could think of was what that would do to your freight allowance! I'm glad it's not true. But I think you hit upon a very important point when you said that you had no obligations [to the embassy]. You were free.

CHILD: We were free to live a normal life. That was the nice thing about being down in the middle ranks, which we always were. And in Germany, we had a boss whom we called Wooden Head the First, and his assistant was Wooden Head the Second. The man who was in charge of the whole thing was an alcoholic and so was his wife. Paul's favorite thing was "Eye on Target" and you didn't feel that anyone had EOT there. They were all trying to get ahead, and you had no feeling that anyone had much of any purpose, except for the younger people who were all full of idealism and so forth on the whole. But the upper ones were people you did not admire, and I think it's horrid working for people you don't admire.

FENZI: Do you realize that taking a cultural phenomena and making it your own really makes you a role model for the young women today, many of whom are reluctant to go abroad because they have a midlevel management job, I was going to say at a Savings and Loan, but perhaps that is not a good example. [*Laughter*] One of the things we hope to do with the book that will eventually come out of this material, is to show young women that—

CHILD: You can have a wonderful time.

FENZI: A wonderful time. And you can then bring these skills back that you have picked up.

CHILD: And you must learn the language. In those days, before we went over to Germany . . . In those days, it was all slots and bodies—you got someone who was a cultural affairs officer who had the mind of a mechanic, who knew nothing, didn't speak the language. I think that was regrettable, because when you think of the Russian heyday, they had to learn various languages, and I think that in the Foreign Service, you should have two major languages and two minor ones. You should really concentrate on those things so that when you send somebody over they could go right in and talk. Because what good are you if you can't talk to the people? Absolutely none. I think maybe now that we are not top dog, we may begin to take things a little more seriously. I think we always thought that we were so wonderful and that everyone could learn English. But it was interesting as an example, too, when we were in Kunming. At about two o'clock in the morning, the Chinese came around to everybody's compound and said, "We would like you all to stay in. We are having a little revolution." They went, I think, to the Dutch, the English, and the French; nobody knew anything about it. So I think it was probably because we didn't really have people who were speaking Chinese and penetrating in.

FENZI: That's why the China Hands—John Service, John Paton Davies, John Carter Vincent, Edmund Clubb—they were invaluable. [*Fenzi relates having lunch with Jack and Caroline Service in Berkeley. Jack Service, now in his eighties, ordered the meal in flawless Chinese.*]

CHILD: I am glad that he is still around. Was he ever exonerated?

FENZI: Yes, he was.

CHILD: But that was a disgusting era.

FENZI: I think he was out for six years, and then he came back in and was sent to Liverpool. Why were you in Kunming? Was it a listening post way up there?

CHILD: It was just over the border from the Burma Road. So that was our real headquarters, but we were all over China at that point. And Chongqing was still the capital, but it was not the main post. But it was fascinating, there were two or three hundred thousand people. And I remember when they had a fire, the firemen would all dress up in costume with dragons and things and parade around the fire. I don't think they ever put it out. And I have in mind that there are about eleven million people living there in that little town. It's probably changed a lot.

FENZI: Yes, it has. Caroline Service went back in '75 and said she couldn't believe how it had just leapt forward into the twentieth century.

CHILD: Of course, I remember, too, that in our country we were really very isolated in the days before World War II. It was only the very rich or students that would ever get over abroad, and then we got to know it during the war, but it wasn't until air traffic began that we really began going over there. So a lot of people felt that it wasn't necessary to know foreign languages.

FENZI: Since working on this project, I have wondered what the Europeans and Latin Americans and others thought of the United States. Because our diplomats who were going over in the twenties, and even in to the thirties, were [ambassadors] like Joseph Grew and John Campbell White with their own immense personal fortunes. Our noncareer ambassadors are traditionally well heeled, or they wouldn't be there.

CHILD: Well, Chip Bohlen, and did you know Freddy Reinhardt [ambassador to Italy from 1961 to 1968]? Have you talked to Solie Reinhardt? She has a daughter, Aura [Aurelia] Reinhardt, who lives in New York, and Solie lives in Porto Ercole, they built a house there. He was a charming fellow, he was a good friend of ours too. She is just darling, and they have a son I think, and Aura is in one of the big wine companies, and she would know when her mother would be coming over. But she was great fun. When he was in Paris, he was number two I think. And then he was our ambassador to Italy. I think they had to provide Bohlen and Reinhardt . . .

FENZI: Yes, there was congressional legislation to create funds.

CHILD: It seems to me that our present administration has been craven in picking nonprofessionals. It is really disgusting. I think the Europeans would hate it and feel belittled when they got someone who really is not a diplomat. We were back in Norway, and they do have a very nice couple there, it's a woman ambassador, and she is not a career woman but she has had her own career. And I think she is doing very well and is very much concerned. And is someone that you could admire.

FENZI: I keep going back to your ability [to lead your own life]. I really felt that as a Foreign Service wife that I was at the beck and call—Guido was an economic officer and started out as a young officer like everybody else. But it just seemed to me that my first obligation was to [his position at] the embassy. In my spare time in Morocco I collected folktales and Moroccan recipes.

CHILD: I think with us, being in the USIA—it was kind of a step-child, and we were not really considered part of the brotherhood.

FENZI: But you see I always rather envied you because—

CHILD: Because we weren't.

FENZI: You were there to share cultures, and you met the university people.

CHILD: Like in Norway. Norway was such a nice country. You met all the people that you would have wanted to meet anyway.

FENZI: But once you left Paris, you must have spent a great deal of your time refining your recipes and working.

CHILD: Well, just working. I think people just say "recipes," but it's not. It's the conception of what you are trying to do. A book is kind of an organic thing that comes out, and that's what takes so long. And then you have to try and make sense out of things, so that things are not a babel of recipes but an organic growth.

FENZI: Well, you must have done just that. The *New Yorker* article says that previously a French recipe was just a few notes by a chef, who knew exactly what he was doing anyway.

CHILD: Well, if you have had the classic training, all you need are the few notes, because there is a repertoire of *la cuisine* that will say that you do a lobster *à l'américaine*, you make such and such soufflé and such and such sauce. You don't need to have any more directions because you know what they are talking about.

FENZI: And then you improvise and do variations on those themes?

CHILD: Yes. Let's see. Marseille we enjoyed very much because we had that nice ambassador. In Germany, we had only had our three lessons of German . . . or had we gotten up to eight lessons. We had an awfully nice German doctor, and we invited him and his wife over for dinner, and they didn't speak any English at all. It was a heavy evening. [*Laughter*] I think we mutually agreed that we liked each other very much, but we couldn't get along [without a common language]. That was a great handicap. I had time to take more German; I went to the university. We were there for two years, but two years is not enough to learn a language.

Then in Norway, I did very much the same thing. But when we went over last summer, we were doing a television thing, *A Taste of Norway*. I got some cassettes, and I was able to do a little bit. They are always so pleased if you make an effort and can say a little something. But they were just as nice then. I remember when we were over there, we had some [Norwegian] friends who were quite a bit younger than we were, and now they are all in their sixties! We had a very interesting and good time; of course, if you want to make money, you don't go into the diplomatic service. But it is a fascinating time. You were in Sierra Leone and all those places. I think if we had stayed in longer we probably would have ended up in deepest Africa, I'm sure.

FENZI: Well, maybe one post there, who knows. Your husband sounds like a very interesting man.

CHILD: Black belt in judo and photographer and painter. He was not a bureaucratic man. What he liked to do was have his work and do it. And he was never ambitious. I know there were some of them in the Paris embassy who would go in on Sundays and Saturdays, busy work, so people could see they were there. Paul left as soon as he could leave, and did his work, and he just didn't get into the politics of the bureaucracy at all, so he never rose very far.

FENZI: Well, Guido was the same way. I remember once reading one of his efficiency reports, which said that he lacked ambition. There is nothing wrong with not being ambitious if you do your work well. You take your weekends off. I think it is very interesting that he [Paul Child] was willing to be so supportive of you, because he had been very creative and . . .

CHILD: He was still able [to be creative]. If you are a painter, you need long times alone, and if you are doing writing, you need long times alone, so it worked out very nicely. It was so nice to be together all the time. That's what you get married for.

FENZI: So you have had a long life in Cambridge.

CHILD: Thirty-two years. Before we went to Norway we had looked all over and decided that we would live in Cambridge rather than California. California at that point seemed so far away. So we got a wonderful house for $35,000, just almost exchanged our little house in Georgetown for that. Now we couldn't afford to buy it, it's gone up so much. Did you buy this a long time ago?

FENZI: Well, 1977.

CHILD: Just before . . .

FENZI: Yes, we came back from Rotterdam at the right time. If we had come back six months later, we would be out in the suburbs.

CHILD: It's so nice to be right here, isn't it?

FENZI: Oh, yes. And Cambridge must be wonderful. We like Cambridge. It must be a wonderful walking town.

CHILD: We bought an apartment in Montecito Shores, which is right across from the Biltmore [in Santa Barbara]. We are on the third floor, and we look over a meadow and there's the water. So wonderful. In the morning, we walk to the Biltmore to get our newspaper and walk on the beach, and it is just a lovely place. And then you go out and you look, and you say, "Look at those mountains, aren't they beautiful?" It's such a beautiful place.

FENZI: Tell me about the book you have just done now.

CHILD: This is a book called *The Way to Cook*. Presumptuous title chosen by our editor at Knopf. My last TV series was called *Dinner at Julia's*—this was about '82. And then we decided to do six one-hour teaching cassettes, which are called "The Way to Cook." So that was the genesis of it. But before that I was doing a monthly article for *Parade* [magazine]. And it had wonderful photographs, I think every two months or so we would have a photographic session, and so forth, and they very kindly gave us all the photographs they had taken. Beautiful color photographs.

FENZI: I remember some of those.

CHILD: We had to take about a hundred more, so we had about six hundred photographs or more. So that was the sort of bones of the book. Then I decided that rather than doing a regular recipe book that it would be much better to do it by cooking method. The idea being that if you know the technique and the basics, then the rest of the things are just building blocks that you know also, and it's how you put them together. I try to urge people to take that conception of cookery because it makes it so much easier. Then you know that anything you see, you can cook. You don't need recipes. In other words, get things into your computer.

FENZI: And get a screen down in the kitchen.

CHILD: I took so much time getting that book done that I have never had time to help on our American Institute of Wine and Food, which we started about ten years ago. Because quite a number of people are taking the profession very seriously. We have lots of people who have very good educations and quite a few of them who have come from other things like banking or something else besides, and they would much rather be in food and wine. Then it's high time that it should be considered a serious profession and a discipline. And we are, finally, after a long time . . . in Boston University they had a very fine culinary facility, and we have gotten them to agree that we shall have a master's degree in gastronomy. The first course is just going on now. It is very hard to get the academics because the academics don't know anything about the [culinary] profession at all.

They just think it is a lot of little people piddling around in a kitchen and making hamburgers. They don't know that we have culinary historians, and that it is interdisciplinary and so forth. They feel that it is purely artisan. So we say to them, "Well, if you are an architect, you have to get your hands in the building, and if you are a surgeon, you have to get your hands in the body. It's the same thing with gastronomy." So the courses—I don't remember how many—will include aesthetics, communications, marketing, anthropology, sociology, language, oenology, and culinary history.

Yesterday Anne Willan was there, so she and I were doing a seminar on "From Escoffier to Nouvelle Cuisine," which was fun, ending up with just a little bit in the kitchen. Like the Escoffier classic *espagnole* sauce, which took us literally three days to make, but it is absolutely delicious. I kept most of it, and it is in my freezer. Well, it's so nice. We had some left over roast beef, which I just sautéed with some onions and things and then simmered it in a little bit of red wine and finished off with a big spoonful of that *demi-glace* sauce, and there you are. Delicious, easy.

FENZI: If the sauce takes three days, it must have to reduce and reduce and reduce.

CHILD: Well, it's not that. You first start out with a bone. You have to have six kilos of meaty shanks.

FENZI: And a pan like this [*forming a huge circle with her arms*].

CHILD: So we boiled just the bones—they need boiling for about twelve hours—and then that's strained out, and then you have your *mirepoix** and your meat, and the stock goes in again. And then you have to have your brown *roux*† after that, and it goes on and on. But it is delicious. And there are still some classic restaurants that still do it. It makes it so easy to have on hand.

---

* A mixture of vegetables and herbs used to flavor meat and seafood dishes and sauces.

† Mixture of butter (usually) and flour cooked together for varying periods of time, depending on its final use.

FENZI: And you can freeze it.

CHILD: You can freeze it.

FENZI: Reading the profile [in the 1974 *New Yorker*], the amount of work it must have been for you to put on those programs in San Francisco and Seattle.

CHILD: They were fun. I still do it. We've just been doing it. But we always have helpers. I was finally getting gridlock at home, and I called up the Katharine Gibbs school, and I said who I was and what I needed. And they said, "Oh, you know, I think you may be in luck. Because we just have a young woman who graduated from the Culinary Institute of America, and she just graduated from us." I said, "Send her right over." She came right over, and I hired her on the spot. She is just marvelous and that has made a great deal of difference. She helps me, and we have some good old friends who have been with me for years. And we all have a very good time.

FENZI: You were having a good time twenty-five years ago.

CHILD: We had lots of fun, yes. [*Pauses*] The American Institute of Wine and Food, that's mostly what I do now. That, and I am very much interested in Planned Parenthood and Smith College and the Democratic Party—I don't know as much about that as I do about the other things.

FENZI: Planned Parenthood, I think, gets to the root of all of our problems.

CHILD: Oh, my. This new Supreme Court is so disturbing, isn't it? Do you think that they are going to undo everything that has been done?

FENZI: I think so. Look how young they are. They are going to be there forever.

CHILD: And that woman, [Justice] Sandra Day O'Connor! She has been a zero, hasn't she?

FENZI: Total disappointment. I maintain it's her fault that abortion issues have been thrown back to the states, to the state legislatures. What a waste of time.

CHILD: And when you think of France and Italy, this isn't even an issue any more.

FENZI: And it shouldn't be an issue here because the issue is not abortion. It's the woman's right to have control over her own body.

CHILD: Family planning. Then they say, "Killing babies! You're killing babies!" Who wants a baby that is from a crack mother? They wouldn't adopt any of those people. If we had the Planned Parenthood in the schools, then we wouldn't have to have any abortions.

FENZI: [*Cites* Washington Post *article about birth and stabilization costs only of a crack/cocaine baby: $44,000.*]

CHILD: Or even more. It's terrible. [*Looks at watch*] I think I must leave [for a luncheon appointment]. This has been fun, just to talk with you.

FENZI: I do thank you so much for sharing your time with me.

BIOGRAPHICAL DATA

Spouse: Paul Cushing Child

Spouse's Position: OSS (visual presentations), Department of State (graphic designer, information officer, public affairs officer), USIS (information officer, cultural affairs officer, exhibits officer)

Spouse Entered USG: 1943

Left Service: 1960

You Entered USG: Same

Status: Spouse of USIS officer, retired

Posts: Husband:

> OSS: New Delhi, India
> Colombo, Ceylon (Sri Lanka)
> 1943–1945 Kunming, China
>
> Department of State: 1945–1947, Washington, DC
> 1948–1952, Paris, France
> 1953–1954, Marseille, France

USIS: 1954–1956, Bonn, Germany
1956–1958 Washington, DC
1959–1960 Oslo, Norway

Self:

Department of State: 1943, Washington, DC

OSS: 1944–1945, Colombo, Ceylon, and Kunming, China

Place/Date of Birth: Pasadena, California, August 15, 1912

Maiden Name: Julia Carolyn McWilliams

Parents: John McWilliams, manager, family farming lands in Arkansas and Southern California, and Caro McWilliams

Schools:

Katherine Branson School, Ross, California
Smith College, BA, 1934

Professions:

Cook/Author (*Mastering the Art of French Cooking*, volumes I and II, and other books)

Television personality (*The French Chef* and other series)

Date/Place of Marriage: September 3, 1946, Lumberville, Pennsylvania

Volunteer and Paid Positions Held:

Studied and wrote about the art of French cooking in Paris

In Washington, DC, 1943 ("a dreadful typing job in a government information agency laughingly called Mellett's Madhouse by employees"); OSS

BA and honorary degrees from Smith College, Boston University, Bates College

"I'M NOT A CHEF, I'M A TEACHER AND A COOK."

INTERVIEW BY MICHAEL ROSEN
TELEVISION ACADEMY FOUNDATION
JUNE 25, 1999

MICHAEL ROSEN: We had just talked about your appearance on the show on WGBH in 1962 called *I've Been Reading* and because of that show, WGBH received a favorable response. Tell me what happened next.

JULIA CHILD: Well, there were . . . they really had to enlarge their audience. It was very, I think very academic, and it was talking heads most of the time and they wanted to enlarge themselves. So they thought they should do—they began having a science show, and they did some art and so forth, and they asked me if I'd like to do a cooking show segment so I said fine and fortunately they picked young Russell Morash who was then just twenty-seven years old, and he'd been doing the science show, and there was a Ruth Lockwood who had been doing the Mrs. Roosevelt shows and they were both available. And so we decided to do three shows and do things that would catch the general public that were well-known. We decided on French onion soup and coq au vin,—or beef bourguignonne, I don't remember which.

ROSEN: But these were pilot programs?

CHILD: They were pilot programs, just to see whether there really was a response.

ROSEN: I just want to establish that, uh, Russell was the producer of that?

CHILD: Mm-hmm, he was the producer, and Ruth.

ROSEN: And Ruth Lockwood was the associate producer.

CHILD: My—my personal director, he was the overall, and she and I worked out the details together. She was very good, she really had a feeling for television, and also humor, and so we worked out these three shows; we decided, as we said, you have to go on with a bang and you can't go out with a whimper. And they were easy shows to do and it—we did them down in Boston, which was hard to get to and hard to park, but we had to bring everything that we had and bring it down into the basement of . . . uh, I don't know what kind of a place it was, I guess it was a gas company or something . . . um, and we just started in. I had done lots of demonstrations so that was—now that didn't bother me, and luckily and the camera didn't bother me. Some people get awfully conscious of it, but I was always kind of, I think, if you just pay attention to what you're doing then you're not conscious of anything else.

ROSEN: So it was one camera?

CHILD: We either had one or two. I don't remember, oddly enough. I think we had an overhead mirror; I don't even remember that.

ROSEN: The overheard mirror to show, uh, an overshot?

CHILD: Mm-hmm, I think we didn't—no, we didn't have an overhead mirror. I don't know how we showed things; I just tipped them. And those were shows in mid-summer; I remember it was very hot there when we showed the first one down in our garden. We had fans going and it turned out that we did indeed—there was indeed an audience, because at that point, people were interested in cooking and that was before there were two family members working, so that women had time to cook and people really were cooking at home a lot. And it went over really very well, people were really interested, and I think I mentioned before about the Kennedys in the White House.

ROSEN: No, you haven't actually.

CHILD: Oh, well, the Kennedys were in the White House then, and they had their wonderful French chef René Verdon. Everything they did was news! And when they did food, of course, that became news. And at that point, too, you could get over to Europe by plane in a few hours, rather than spending five or six days. Really, the time was right, so we got on at exactly the right point. If it would have been earlier, it wouldn't have gone over, 'cause we wouldn't—the Americans wouldn't have been going abroad. So we knew it was very lucky just hitting it right, and they decided that it was worthwhile so, . . . but it was still experimental, so the first thirteen shows were done on old tape and they were just shown locally, and then it might've been Pittsburgh decided they'd like to do it so they borrowed the tapes, and then San Francisco borrowed them and then—and then, finally, New York did, and we felt we had arrived. So the first thirteen shows don't even exist anymore.

ROSEN: Really?

CHILD: The tape, I guess, the tape must have worn out.

ROSEN: What's the name of the show?

CHILD: It was *The French Chef.* We decided to call it *The French Chef,* because it would fit in one line in the TV guide. And I had hoped also at that point that we'd get some real French chefs to come in, which of course we never did but it was about French classical,—French cooking. And it was entirely classical French cooking, which was—which I'm glad it was. And we . . . then those went over well, so we did thirteen more.

ROSEN: I want to stop you here and ask about the format of the show. How long was the show itself?

CHILD: They were always half-hour, so I think it was twenty-seven minutes when you took out the, you know, the beginnings and the ends and the WGBH things, so we had twenty-seven minutes and we didn't stop at all unless something awful happened, if everything fell on the floor or whoops, whatnot, like there'd be an electricity problem, but they just went. And they really got a lot in real time and we hadn't developed our system of having one or two ready at various stages.

ROSEN: So it, uh, there's no editing involved?

CHILD: There was no editing at all, and you see some of the old shows now, they seem endlessly long, with all the stirring and so forth.

ROSEN: Would you, over the course of one show, just make one dish, or would you do multiple?

CHILD: It was often just one dish so that we could really go into detail with exactly how we'd make the sauce and so forth, and we always felt that less was more. And we did have some that were dinners in half an hour, which we did in three courses, but otherwise it was really just one dish and how to do it.

ROSEN: Now in my times cooking in the kitchen, I know that some dishes take longer than half an hour, how did you . . . how'd you get over that problem?

CHILD: Well, that was when we knew if we were doing a stew then we'd have one ready, and as we went along we'd hover on what was ready so that you could see up to a certain point then, *here's how it looks now.* By the magic of television, we just said you let it cook until it looks like this. So then we could do stews and braises and everything else.

ROSEN: How did you know how much time you had left?

CHILD: That was a problem that we, I think in the third—the third show, which was French onion soup, when we were doing the three trials, we found that I didn't have any feeling for time and there was so much to do in that show and I was just galloping through it. We found that we had eight minutes left; we did it over and the same problem happened so we changed the system of having idiot cards, they said, you know, "move the spoon." We divided it up into sections and I could have as long as I wanted in one section, and then we'd move to the next one, so that fixed the timing.

ROSEN: So someone would be off-camera with cue cards and a stopwatch?

CHILD: Well, Ruthie Lockwood was always right there, she was very good at that. She knew exactly what we were doing, so she'd pass up something to the floor manager who would hold it under the camera and I would see it, and that worked extremely well. But that disastrous one when I was galloping through and had so much time left—

ROSEN: Tell me about that.

CHILD: Well, that was the French onion soup one, where I had so much to do and I was going very fast and did it all too fast, and we came up to the end and I had eight minutes left with nothing to do but talk. So we wiped that out and developed our new system, which worked out very well. And in those days—this was before, before you had the monitors that fit right over the lens, and these, you had to have an idiot card, and you can definitely see some of these guys go down with an idiot card and come up again.

ROSEN: How, um, I'm assuming—because television, public television is notorious for not having much money—that you didn't have much of a budget.

CHILD: No, we had very little budget and I think I was paid fifty dollars a show. Well, PBS never pays much of anything. And what we would do, we would auction things off—say if we had a steak show, we would auction off the steaks afterwards, but usually we ate everything, so that was nice. [*Laughs*]

ROSEN: But also, I mean, I would assume that because of all the fresh ingredients you needed and considering you had to, if you're showing how to cook duck, you have to have a couple ducks, that gets expensive. How would you do it?

CHILD: Well, I guess, I don't remember, but I guess we definitely had a budget.

ROSEN: And then what about all the pots and pans?

CHILD: Paul and I did all the shopping, and then we gradually bought pots and pans as we went along. At first, they were all mine which we'd bring over, but I don't know . . . I don't remember now how the expenses went. But we were never—never extravagant, certainly. And very often we would have—raising money for GBH, we would have an audience come in. I remember when we were doing tripe. There's—one of the good things about public television was that we could throw things that a commercial station never would, like tripe wouldn't have enough appeal, but it was fun seeing the big piece of tripe, a big raw piece, looked like a shaggy rug. It was interesting; we had older people and we had a bunch of young people in that came from the school, and when we passed it around for people to taste it, older people just went "no." All the younger ones wanted to eat it and try it out, but people weren't very adventurous then. In our crew, a lot of the crew had never eaten a fresh artichoke, or never eaten fresh asparagus; it was interesting that at that point people didn't—weren't very adventurous. But there wasn't that much offered. But imagine not ever eating fresh asparagus, for instance.

ROSEN: It was always canned, or . . . ?

CHILD: Yes, I don't know what, 'cause I—we never ate that, but the general public evidently did. So we really taught a lot of people things. There weren't any leeks anywhere until we began showing them, and we found also that a lot of the markets began finding out what we were doing and then they would stock what we had. Williams-Sonoma, the cookware store, was very useful to us 'cause anything that,—we had oval perforated metal egg poachers, if you know how hard it is to get an egg, poached egg, to look, and you can find these little oval metal things, and I have some here, and you drop the egg into it and then it keeps its shape. And then, you know, we then began to find them around and then—it was interesting about the egg poacher—then people said eggs were dangerous, you know, back then people didn't have eggs, even two a day, so the egg poachers were back in. That's odd, isn't it?

ROSEN: It is. So Williams-Sonoma started getting requests for certain cookery?

CHILD: Yes, they were very, very helpful because they would carry these things—they had a lot of very good things that I would like to use. I liked to show new things like a salad dryer, like it spins like in a basket, and it has—at least the one I have—has this string and you pull it and it rotates 'round and 'round and all the water is thrown off, and I think our show was the first place that it was shown. And then also, the use of a blowtorch, which is very useful if you want to . . . you could unmold—say, for if you have a gelatin dessert, and you want to unmold it, you have to take a blowtorch and run it around just to loosen it and then it unmolds very easily. Or you can brown something nicely with it. I think we were the first to use that.

ROSEN: And a lot of these techniques and the cookery, you got from France.

CHILD: Yes, they were all French, but some of them were mine. At least we showed a lot about knives and utensils and it was always fun having funny things, like I have a great big knife which I call "fright knife". [*Gestures*] It's about that long, about that wide, and jagged edges on it. It does look very dangerous. And we were the first people to use the food processor when we produced it on the TV. So it was very useful for people to know it was out there.

ROSEN: And it certainly fell in line with what WGBH stood for, and certainly public television: education.

CHILD: And what's nice was—I said, it was nice that you could show things like tripe, and also you can go into detail. I know, I'm very much interested in the Food Network, but they have a difficulty because they have to make money, so they have to have entertainment, and they really can't have the kind of serious teaching shows that we can have on PBS. Because the audience attention is short.

ROSEN: Well, I want stay with *The French*, uh, *Chef*, here, and I didn't mention that the first episode of *The French Chef* aired on January 23, 1963, and it was a Monday evening, eight o'clock, it aired.

CHILD: Mm-hmm. We had a wonderful hour, I wish we still had that.

ROSEN: It's the prime time.

CHILD: Monday at eight, that's primetime. That was wonderful.

ROSEN: What did the set look like?

CHILD: Well, the set looked just like a kitchen. It was all open; you just had a counter in the front, with a counter here, and then enough room so that you could stand and move around and then in the back of the room was the sink and work spaces. So it looked like a kitchen. You almost had a window, and there was something to look at outside, like a tree, so it looked like a kitchen.

ROSEN: And tell me briefly: the preparation for a show. How many shows a week did you shoot?

CHILD: Well, the first—I don't know how we did it; it seemed to me that we did four shows a week. You know, it's so long ago, it was over thirty-five years ago; I kind of forget what we did. [*Laughs*] But of course, I knew everything very well because I'd done it all. But we would have to do all the shopping. At first, Paul and I did all the shopping. And we didn't really practice, but Ruth and I would always work it out together and then shoot it. It was wonderful having Russ, because he was always full of ideas and his family were cooks, and his wife was a cook, so that helped a lot. But we would have to set it up and sort of just go right to it—in a way, it's rather the way Jacques Pepin and I did the *Cooking at Home*, in which we had all the stuff out and we just cooked. We were making two a day, easily, with that setup, at least. We were able to do two a day, twice a week. If you know what you're doing and it's not—and it's fairly simple—it's possible to do, and I think, at *The Food Network*, they do. Emeril Lagasse, does more than that, probably.

ROSEN: I like watching him. Speaking of which, I mean, back in '62, '63 . . . this was a brand new thing. People had never seen something like this before.

CHILD: No, they hadn't.

ROSEN: How did you make cooking educational but also interesting and dramatic and make people watch?

CHILD: Well, I think cooking is—it's kind of a drama any-way, because you start with nothing and you end up with something to eat. And I'm, luckily, I'm a natural ham, and I think that helps. And I don't get flustered because I'm not doing anything that I don't know how to do. So, we made it fun because I was having a good time, and that makes a lot of difference. And I wasn't doing anything that I didn't know about.

ROSEN: And you love food.

CHILD: I love food and I enjoyed it.

ROSEN: You mention humor, too. How important is humor?

CHILD: Well, I think it's very important. You can't—it has to be a natural humor, I think; it has to come out of what you're doing.

ROSEN: Now I want to also ask this: was this show live or was it . . . it was taped?

CHILD: It was taped. It was live, it was really live on tape because we didn't stop, we went right through. But of course which we now don't do, now we do it in segments.

ROSEN: That's different.

CHILD: Yeah, very different. And there was always a kind of breathless—is it really going to turn out? You don't quite know. Which I think has a certain charm, to get all this done in twenty-seven minutes.

ROSEN: Who were the sponsors of the first *French Chef*?

CHILD: I think, the first one I think we had—I know we had Polaroid, I think Polaroid was at the very beginning. It seemed to me there was a market; I don't remember. Luckily, I don't have to do anything at all about getting sponsors. That's what you want, as I understand, is—the first thing is to get a producer and the producer gets the sponsors.

ROSEN: Well, would it have mattered what kind of sponsor?

CHILD: Yes, I wouldn't do anything for a product I didn't like. Like I don't believe in bottled salad dressing, so I would not want a bottled salad dressing doing the show.

ROSEN: Still to this day you don't like bottled salad dressing?

CHILD: Well, why should you have it bottled? It's so easy to make. And they never use very good oil.

ROSEN: That makes sense. Um, now as you mentioned, another thirteen episodes were added, and then by 1965, *The French Chef* was seen in ninety-six stations around the country.

CHILD: Mm-hmm, I think almost everyone carried it then. We'd been—we weren't clever enough to have a book tag on it, so it never advertised our book, which everything does now. That was too bad, but I unfortunately am not a very good business woman, and we never thought of that.

ROSEN: Well, I think you've done pretty well. How was *The French Chef* received by critics? Remember?

CHILD: I don't know, did they even pay attention to it? I'm not sure, I don't know. I remember when we did *Dinner at Julia's*, there must have been some kind of a depression but we had; it was supposed to be a real dinner party, this was out in Santa Barbara, and some of the boys at the UC Santa Barbara had an old Rolls Royce which we borrowed and we had to push into the set. We were criticized for having a Rolls Royce in such harsh times.

ROSEN: 1965 was a very good year to you; you received a Peabody award and an Emmy, in fact. It was the first educational television show . . . actually, you, personally, to win an award.

CHILD: As you could always tell, if you went to one of these events, you had television people, and public television has always been at the very bottom of everything. You could tell, if anyone was sitting next to you, that they were probably on their way out. [*Laughs*] So that was kind of—we knew it was the kiss of death.

ROSEN: Now, who were the major chefs at that time, in the mid-sixties here? You've mentioned a chef for Kennedy.

CHILD: That was really before, before chefs became so popular as they are now. People didn't know, really, much about them; you knew more the name of the restaurant, but you didn't know the name of the chef. I think—was that before Paul Prudhomme started out? Oh yeah, I think he was getting famous by then. We didn't have so many American chefs then. Well, they would be foreigners who were here.

ROSEN: But it's traditionally been a man's profession.

CHILD: It has.

ROSEN: And here you were, not only—

CHILD: But I'm not a chef; I'm a teacher and a cook. So that's quite different. But in France, there's still—cooking is not a woman's profession at all, and it's very hard to find women in the profession, oddly enough.

ROSEN: Why?

CHILD: Because they don't take it as a serious discipline, and they're not welcome.

ROSEN: We were talking about *The French Chef*, the first show, *The French Chef*, which ran from 1963 to '66. Now, this show was in black and white.

CHILD: This show, that was before color was invented. And we really had—I think we had two cameras at the most at that time. And it wasn't until . . . I can't remember what the date was, that color suddenly came in. And we had never seen color at all in our house, and they had a big national meeting of public television stations, and they had—they were showing—they had one color camera and they had a black-and-white camera, and they had them side by side. And they had everyone come in to do their shows just a little bit. I remember I did a strawberry tart, and I did a *salade niçoise*, and I did a blanquette veal, and it was like night and day. The *blanquette* veal was different shades of grey, then in color you could suddenly see the subtle difference between the veal and the sauce. And of course the salade niçoise was a riot of color with green and tomatoes and so forth and beans. And we went home right afterwards and got a colored television. That was just . . . it was like . . . it was amazing, the difference. And that was . . . I can't remember when color came out.

ROSEN: Well, I have it here that you didn't have color until 1970 on the second *French Chef* show.

CHILD: Yes, mm-hmm.

ROSEN: The first show was in black and white.

CHILD: Yep. The first 119 were all in black and white. That little book I held, *The French Chef Cookbook*, was a very nice little précis of French classical cooking, that was all black and white.

ROSEN: Did you have to do anything differently to the food to make it more appealing?

CHILD: No, no. But we had my nice friend Rosemary, who was our food developer. We didn't call her "stylist"; she was "food designer." But she was very conscious of that, too. We always had a beauty shot at the beginning and at the end.

ROSEN: I forgot to mention whether you remember the first time you saw television? And what you thought of it.

CHILD: Well, we'd been living abroad. So we hadn't really seen any television at home when we—our last foreign post was in Norway, and we came home in, I guess it was '56. So we got ourselves a little black—a little television. They were all black and white. And that was the first time we ever saw it.

ROSEN: What'd you think of it? Did you think it would . . . ?

CHILD: It was wonderful. We didn't see . . . it was mostly the news that we saw. *Huntley-Brinkley*, they had at that time. They were wonderful on the news.

ROSEN: Did you ever think that you would be on television?

CHILD: No, I didn't think of it at all. I didn't ever do any planning of doing this or that. I just . . . I happened to fall into it on the whole. If it happened to be the right person at the right time, you're very lucky.

ROSEN: In 1966, *The French Chef* went off the air for four years. Why was that?

CHILD: I guess I was doing something else. I don't remember. And then we came back with . . .

ROSEN: Well, you had *The French Chef Cookbook*. You published *The French Chef Cookbook*.

CHILD: Mm-hmm. And then we did volume two of *Mastering*. That probably—that probably took a lot of time, I imagine. Then we came on again with *Julia Child and Company*. We had two series of that. And then, then we went out to Santa Barbara and what was that called?

ROSEN: Uh, *Dinners at*—

CHILD: *Dinner at Julia's*! That was fun.

ROSEN: Well that's in '83. So I'm not going to let you go there yet.

CHILD: Oh, all right.

ROSEN: I just want to get a couple more specifics on *The French*

Chef. As we mentioned, the second show, *The French Chef,* which premiered in 1970, was in color. Um, did that make any difference to you in regards to how you did the show?

CHILD: No. No, not at all.

ROSEN: How many people were working for you at this point?

CHILD: Well just on my team alone, we always had—it was Ruth, and me, and we had Rosie, the food designer. And we had Liz, who was kind of head, we had a group called dishwashers who also were, who did everything else. We had about eight people, I think. In the kitchen, we had . . . Marian Morash at one time was our executive chef. That was when we planned to have definitely things in various stages, like if it was a stew there was a second stage and the third and so forth. So we had about eight people, I think.

ROSEN: Did you have associate cooks to help?

CHILD: Yes, so that was the executive chef and then her associates, usually two or three.

ROSEN: And, you had Polaroid as the sponsor as well?

CHILD: Polaroid was our *first* sponsor. I don't remember who the other ones were. It seemed to me we had Safeway at one point? I had nothing to do with the sponsorship. I think Russ did that.

ROSEN: And I see here that you shot some episodes in France?

CHILD: That was fun. Well, we . . . Gosh, it was not Russ that was with us, it was some,—another director. We went to Marseilles and showed the fish markets, and we were in Paris and we did some shots with Professor Calvel when we were doing French bread and baguettes and things; that was wonderful. And we had some . . . a wonderful pastry chef. Went to several restaurants. That was . . . those were fun to do.

ROSEN: So you really let some air into television there.

CHILD: Yes, we did.

ROSEN: Which I don't think was ever done before.

CHILD: That I don't know. But that was great fun. I'm glad we did that.

ROSEN: But only a year later that show was canceled. Why was that? Do you remember why?

CHILD: What show? What series?

ROSEN: *The French Chef.* The second *French Chef* was canceled.

CHILD: Maybe I was doing another book.

ROSEN: But it wasn't . . . it wasn't because of WGBH or anything?

CHILD: No, I think anytime, I just canceled it. And I did, let's see, I did *Julia Child's Kitchen*. I think the first time it was canceled was when I was doing volume two of *Mastering*. With a book like that, it takes your whole time.

ROSEN: So, it really, you remained in control of the shows and the books were demanding enough that you couldn't do, really, both.

CHILD: Well, you can't. If you're going to do a really serious book, you can't do anything else. At least I can't.

ROSEN: And '77, you—as you mentioned, *Julia Child and Company* was also produced by Russ Morash.

CHILD: Mm-hmm.

ROSEN: And Ruth Lockwood. And as I understand, it had a much bigger set, bigger crew.

CHILD: Yes, we had our whole building then, which was wonderful, because before we'd always had to set up every time. But when we had our own building, we could have things in the fridge. It was—everything was much, much easier.

ROSEN: And was this also French cooking?

CHILD: Well, my background is always French, but we were just doing regular cooking.

ROSEN: "Regular" as in American or, like, American recipes?

CHILD: Well, it wasn't classical French, so it was . . . it was just cooking.

ROSEN: And at this point you were also, as I noticed—you started writing for magazines. *McCall's.*

CHILD: Yes, I did an article for *McCall's* for several years, and then we did a monthly one for *Parade Magazine.* That was fun. *McCall's* was nice, but it was kind of ladylike, and at the—for *Parade Magazine* I could do whatever we wanted. I liked very much the editor there and the people we worked with. That was—they really did very well on the photographs. And then when I did my book, called *The Way to Cook*— which was a great book, I think. It has wonderful pictures in it—they were very kind. They gave me all these how-to photographs that we'd use, and I'm forever grateful because we never would've written the book if they hadn't been so kind. They were awfully nice to work with.

ROSEN: That always makes the job easier.

CHILD: Oh, yes.

ROSEN: And you mentioned briefly about your appearing on *Good Morning America.* You became a regular on *Good Morning America*!

CHILD: Yes, I was. I enjoyed that very much. We were . . .

what was his name? David? [*thinking*] Hm. I can't remember his name. Who was the male anchor?

ROSEN: Um . . . David Hartman?

CHILD: David Hartman! Yeah, he was there first. And then Charlie Gibson, whom I just love. I enjoyed being with him very, very much.

ROSEN: And do you occasionally continue to appear on there?

CHILD: Once in a long while. I suppose we will probably appear when our new book comes out. Well, I think they would—when I came in, which was nice for me—they'd put me up in the hotel, and I would have some per diem, and they would pay my way, and I think they just found it too expensive.

ROSEN: But you enjoyed that?

CHILD: Oh, very much. Very much. It was awfully nice just to have a paid visit in New York. I loved that.

ROSEN: And, now, did you have a contract with WGBH at all? I mean, you were able to jump to commercial television here on ABC.

CHILD: No, we never had a contract and I think—I guess we had one with ABC. But I have a very nice family lawyer and he took care of all of that. We must've had a contract.

ROSEN: And, now, Paul continued to work very closely with you on—

CHILD: Yes. He had retired by that point. He was a paid-to-earn photographer so he could spend as much time with me as he liked. We were always together, which was very nice.

ROSEN: That's ideal.

CHILD: Yes, he was a supporting advisor, and—he was wonderful.

ROSEN: And you mentioned also in *Dinner at Julia's* in 1983, that's where you hosted dinner parties in Santa Barbara.

CHILD: Yes. We had Jim Beard, and we had all the wine-makers. Everyone had a California winemaker, and that was very nice, I think. Well, I always had wine in the show, which I think is so necessary. I remember once, for red wine, when it was in the black-and-white days, you couldn't see whether it was red or white so we always used Gravy Master in water for red wine and I said—we were having something, and I said—'And now we're going to serve a *château gravie mastère!*' Nobody noticed that at all. [*Laughs*] That always pleased me very much. [*Laughs.*]

ROSEN: Now *Dinner at Julia's* was thirteen episodes. Why always thirteen episodes?

CHILD: Well, if you want a full year you have fifty-six. Then half, of course, is twenty-three or whatever it is. Or fifty-two and half is twenty-six and thirteen is a quarter. It was always divided up in the weeks.

ROSEN: But why not fifty-six?

CHILD: How many weeks are there in the year?

ROSEN: I mean, why not a full schedule?

CHILD: Well it would depend on how much time we wanted to spend.

ROSEN: But you seemed to always limit it to about thirteen shows and I'm just wondering.

CHILD: No, it's always just because it's a quarter of a year. You do either thirteen, twenty-six, or fifty-two, or whatever it is.

ROSEN: But you never wanted to continue a show for a few years?

CHILD: That long? No, because I was doing other things as well. So I was never a complete TV person. I was always a writer as well.

ROSEN: Did you watch TV at this point? Did you have favorite shows?

CHILD: I look at the news only. And once in a while, if I happened to be alone for the evening, I'll watch. I saw a program last night on Channel 33 here, it was . . . who's that? Stephen King who was in an automobile accident?

ROSEN: Just recently? Uh huh.

CHILD: Just recently. It was one of his shows. I can't remember the name of it. A very gloomy one. Well, I'm very glad I saw that last night. [*Laughs*]

ROSEN: Was it a little scary?

CHILD: No. It wasn't scary. It was upsetting. There was a woman who had a horrible husband who beat her, and I don't know why she stayed. I guess she stayed with him because she had no money and no place to go. And he was very brutal, and he was chasing her and he stumbled into a rotting well. And she could've helped save him, but she stood there in horror as it fell and then it fell again, and there was the end. But he had been horribly brutal to her, so she let him die.

ROSEN: You ruined the movie for me. [*Laughs*]

CHILD: And then, there was an upper-class woman for whom she worked. And she had told the woman—she was sobbing one day when she was supposed to be polishing the silver—she finally told the woman that her husband had gone into the savings account, and she had painfully paid in forty dollars a month and had about five thousand dollars she was going to use to send her daughter to college, and he had stolen it all.

And the woman helped her, so when the woman herself began to fail, she went to help her. She was really failing so much, that she wanted to commit suicide. And this, our heroine was charged with the murder. But the woman had thrown herself down the stairs. It was quite gloomy, as you can see.

ROSEN: [*laughs*] It sounds very gloomy. Did you watch the whole thing last night?

CHILD: I did.

ROSEN: [*laughs*] Ah, well there's so many books here, there's so many specials, but I just want to hit on some of the key ones here—

CHILD: I think, well, the main reason that I would stop was that I was doing another book, or I was doing a *Parade* thing or something like that. Well, that meant, I didn't—I had no intention of being a complete television person. It was too limiting.

ROSEN: Why's that?

CHILD: I also wanted to write.

ROSEN: You enjoyed writing at this point?

CHILD: Yeah. And television never paid much.

ROSEN: Do you enjoy watching yourself on television?

CHILD: I look at it once in a while. I don't look very much—I look at one cooking show, usually. I don't—I don't look at them very much. I'll look at some—a weird story like this one, or the news, always. I'm a news freak.

ROSEN: In 1993, there was a show called *Cooking with Master Chefs* on PBS.

CHILD: Mmm, yes.

ROSEN: Tell me about that.

CHILD: That was when I met our new producer Geoff Drummond, whom I like very much. And he was serious about food and about television, and I've always wanted to bring some real professional chefs into the picture. And he was interested in that too, so that's how we managed that. And I think it's wonderful for people to be able to see the real pros.

ROSEN: You don't consider yourself a real pro?

CHILD: I'm a home cook, not a restaurant cook. There's a tremendous difference, and you can see it very clearly in our Jacques Pepin shows. I mean, he is—he is just a remarkable pro. He cooks so fast and so perfectly in everything. And I take my time because I can, but if you're a professional chef, you have to work very fast. And if you're really good, you can work very well and very fast the way he can.

ROSEN: So it's the efficiency?

CHILD: I mean, he can cut up a chicken in about eight seconds. He and Martin Yan have contests to see who can do it faster. It takes me about five minutes; I take my time and I enjoy doing it. I don't care how long it takes. So there's a great, *great* difference.

ROSEN: Well, in the same year that *Cooking with Master Chefs* was produced, which was also thirteen episodes, something called the Food Network was launched. Now, thirty years, virtually, after you started *The French Chef,* someone finally got the idea that it might be a good thing to do. Were you involved with the launching of the Food Network?

CHILD: A little bit. They took all of Dione Lucas, the early first television cook, they took all of hers. Then I think they bought some of the—well, they bought a group of ours, I don't know which ones. And I've been on it several times; I've always been very much interested in hoping it would work. I think they're having a difficult time because they have to get a big audience, and if you're going to be serious and then not just amusing . . . I mean with Emeril Lagasse, all of our gas station attendants, they just adore him, but they're looking it at for fun and amusement, just the way they look at *The Frugal Gourmet.* But they're not going to watch a serious thing on how to debone a turkey or something like that. They want entertainment.

ROSEN: How do you draw that line, though? If the average viewer is watching television, and watching your show for example, um—

CHILD: Well, we don't have an average viewer. We have people who want to learn how to cook, which is quite different from people who just want to be amused by cooking. But our shows are definitely teaching shows, and they're not going to look at a teaching show unless they're interested in the subject. I don't think—at least, I would direct myself to people who want to learn to cook. And that's quite different than just being, having fun.

ROSEN: So what's your audience been? What are your demographics?

CHILD: People who like to cook. They're from all walks of life. I have a lot of men, and I imagine now that we have two parts of the family working that a lot of people aren't really going into serious cooking, except those who really love it as a hobby or want to go into it professionally. There's so many . . . where you go into a market today, there are ready-made foods, and you can take home and cook them or you can take home and sauté them because they're all cut-up. So it's quite different.

ROSEN: Have you always—did you always see these shows as educational, and treated them as such?

CHILD: Yes, I mean, they're teaching shows, very definitely, because I'm not interested otherwise.

ROSEN: You had mentioned earlier about how cooking itself is dramatic and how you add humor, and those are elements of entertainment.

CHILD: But I don't add it for entertainment at all. It's just, I don't consciously entertain anyone. I'm consciously teaching them. But, I'm entertaining myself by cooking, so maybe that comes across.

ROSEN: So it comes out of the process?

CHILD: It comes out of the process. But they're serious teaching shows. And, you wouldn't really look at it unless you wanted to learn something, I think.

ROSEN: Now in '94, you started in a two-hour PBS special, *Julia Child and Jacques Pepin*—

CHILD: Yes.

ROSEN: —*Cooking in Concert.*

CHILD: *Cooking in Concert.*

ROSEN: You did two of those, right?

CHILD: And it's out of that that our new series has come.

ROSEN: What's that called?

CHILD: It's called *Jacques and Julia Cooking at Home.*

THE LAST INTERVIEW

INTERVIEW BY WILBERT JONES
PREPARED FOODS
SEPTEMBER 1, 2004

It was over forty years ago that Julia Child stepped into Americans' homes via television and forever changed their culinary lives. Her message was a simple one: "Use the freshest and finest ingredients to cook with (which does not mean the most expensive). And, if you can't find the right quality ingredients for that dish, pick another recipe."

Julia raised the food consciousness of Americans by urging them to go to their grocery stores and demand better quality ingredients. Nowadays, these foods are basic staples and can be found in any supermarket in America.

This April, her friend and *Prepared Foods*'s contributing writer, Wilbert Jones, visited Child at her home. In what turned out to be her last interview, she spoke with as much passion about food as when her first cooking show aired in 1963. Child passed away in her sleep on August 13, two days shy of her ninety-second birthday. To the end, Child maintained her *bon vivant* image. When asked about her guilty pleasures, she would respond, "I don't have any guilt."

JONES: How has cooking in America evolved?

CHILD: Although I am not an historian and have not done any research in this area, it seems to me that Americans are much more aware of fine cuisine than they were when I first began my career. With the advent of television and the ease of airline travel, Americans have become more exposed to many different types of food. The supermarkets all are providing wonderful, delicious ingredients, and the restaurants are featuring all kinds of ethnic influences in their cuisine. It is wonderful.

JONES: What's available now versus twenty-five years ago— hard-to-find, good-quality ingredients?

CHILD: When I first began my television series on educational television way back in the 1960s, ingredients such as garlic and white button mushrooms were considered exotic. They had to be purchased at specialty stores or at ethnic markets. Now you can walk into the corner convenience store, and there are about twenty-seven kinds of mushrooms! Due to transportation and storage improvements, most "in-season" items are available year-round. We have fruits and vegetables being flown in from around the world. And, through education and travel experiences, the American public is much more knowledgeable about an enormous array of foods and flavors. So, just about everything is available from somewhere [at any time].

JONES: What's your opinion on food products in the grocery stores?

CHILD: Grocery stores do a wonderful job of providing top-quality products. Many of the stores do beautiful displays.

And the "ready-to-go" convenience of already trimmed broccoli, carrots, and other vegetables is great if your time is very limited.

JONES: What are your favorite food ingredients?

CHILD: As long as the items are fresh and flavorful, they are my favorites!

JULIA CHILD was born in 1912 in Pasadena, California. After attending Smith College, she joined the Office of Strategic Services (now the Central Intelligence Agency) where she facilitated top-secret communications between U.S. government officials and intelligence officers during World War II. While stationed in Sri Lanka, she met fellow OSS employee Paul Child, and the two married after the war. In 1948, the couple moved to Paris, where Child attended the famous cooking school Le Cordon Bleu. Her first book, *Mastering the Art of French Cooking*, was published in 1961, was an instant bestseller, and is now a revered classic. In 1962, she launched the first live cooking show, *The French Chef.* From the 1960s through the 1990s, she starred in many television shows and published more than a dozen critically acclaimed books. She is widely recognized as one of the most influential figures in American cooking. She died of kidney failure in Montecito, California, in 2004.

MARTHA DEANE was the radio persona of journalist Marian Young Taylor, who hosted *The Martha Deane* show on WOR from 1941 until 1974 and interviewed more than ten thousand guests, including President Dwight D. Eisenhower, Eleanor Roosevelt, and Fred Astaire. Among her many honors was the Broadcast Pioneers Distinguished Service Award, which she won in 1968. She died on December 9, 1973.

SHARON HUDGINS is the food editor of European Traveler website, the columnist for *German Life* magazine (U.S.), and a regular contributor of food, travel, and cultural articles to several websites and print publications, including *Saveur*, *Gastronomica*, and *National Geographic Traveler*.

POLLY FROST is a writer and performer in New York City. She is the author of *With One Eye Open* and *Deep Inside*, and the coauthor of *The Bannings*. Her work has appeared in the *New Yorker*, *The Atlantic*, *The New York Times*, and many other publications.

JEWELL FENZI is the former wife of an American diplomat, and the author of two memoirs and a cookbook.

MICHAEL ROSEN is a director, producer, and former production executive for the Television Academy.

WILBERT JONES is the president of the Wilbert Jones Company, a Chicago-based food product development and marketing company, founded in 1993.